# The tragedy of the Klondike : this book of travels gives the true facts of what took place in the gold-fields under British rule

Luella Day

**Nabu Public Domain Reprints:**

You are holding a reproduction of an original work published before 1923 that is in the public domain in the United States of America, and possibly other countries. You may freely copy and distribute this work as no entity (individual or corporate) has a copyright on the body of the work. This book may contain prior copyright references, and library stamps (as most of these works were scanned from library copies). These have been scanned and retained as part of the historical artifact.

This book may have occasional imperfections such as missing or blurred pages, poor pictures, errant marks, etc. that were either part of the original artifact, or were introduced by the scanning process. We believe this work is culturally important, and despite the imperfections, have elected to bring it back into print as part of our continuing commitment to the preservation of printed works worldwide. We appreciate your understanding of the imperfections in the preservation process, and hope you enjoy this valuable book.

# THE TRAGEDY
# OF THE KLONDIKE

# The
# TRAGEDY
## of the
# KLONDIKE;

—⋇—

This Book of Travels Gives the True
Facts of What Took Place in
the Gold-fields Under
British Rule

*By*
LUELLA DAY

NEW YORK
1906

COPYRIGHT, 1906, BY LUELLA DAY.

THE AUTHOR.

# This Book is Dedicated

**To** *Those who fell by the wayside and whose bones whiten under the eternal snow of the ice-bound north.*

**To** *Those who mourn their dead lost on the trail.*

**To** *Those who, like myself, survived the hardships and the perils of the quest for gold in the Klondike.*

---

*Not one statement herein contained is false or exaggerated. I have "nothing extenuated nor aught set down in malice," but append to this my solemn oath as to the truth of every statement contained in these pages.*

*rn to before me
's Twenty-fist day of
ember, 1906.
York City, N. Y.*

*Luella Day*

*J. A. Graves*

# PREFACE

FROM time immemorial the human race has been more or less "gold-mad." The lust of gold has been the motive-power which has ruled the world, opened up new countries, made cities to spring up on the plains, discovered new continents, made wars and bloodshed in every part of the world.

Solomon could not have built his temple without gold. It was the motive-power that led to the search for golden fleece. It was the lust for gold that brought Christopher Columbus across a trackless waste of water to discover a new world and a new people and finally to death in chains.

Australia, with its vast area and varied resources, would still be a sheep-farm except for the discovery of auriferous deposits, which was but a penal colony instead of the world-power it is to-day. India was and is the most brilliant of Great Britain's crown-jewels as a producer of gold and precious stones. And all this has been acquired by the few, and the multitude has fallen by the wayside. Men have risked and lost their lives in desert amid thirst and sand-storm; have climbed almost inaccessible heights and perished by the many risks which beset the explorer. And none of these things either daunt or deter men from the quest of the precious, glittering, golden lure, hidden in the bowels of the earth.

In the ages whose history is unwritten lie the tragedies of the gold-lust. The Aztecs, with their primitive methods of roasting the ore, accumulated vast stores of the yellow metal, which with fire and bloodshed the Spaniards took from them, and they went to their graves without revealing the source of their wealth, which remains in great part the secret and the mystery of the land of the Aztec, our next-door neighbor.

When the Aleutian Islands were found to produce gold in quantities, their remote and almost inaccessible location in Behring's Strait did not deter the gold-hunter from his quest any more than did the search for the yellow metal yield to the risks of tropical fevers and deadly reptiles.

This being briefly a true history of the world's mining fever, a disease for which there is not and never will be a remedy, we come naturally to the latest craze and one of the most remarkable. The discovery of placer-gold and the rush for the region in the far Northwest, the Klondike, a much larger population and a greater number of adventurous spirits combined to make the rush excel that which invaded California in the historic days of " '49."

It had been many years since a great gold discovery had been given to the world, when in 1897 the Klondike discovery was given in its primitive form to the world at large.

It was in the autumn of 1898 that the world, or that portion of it which is interested in mining, first heard of the great gold discovery or field in what has since come to be known as the Yukon Territory.

Two prospectors claim credit for the discovery at the same time, though as for time they had no timepieces or almanacs. It was early spring, however, and the two prospectors were camped about sixty miles apart. These men were prospectors from boyhood, trained only as a hunting-dog is broken.

They are a unique class of men. They go out every year with never-dying hope and supply of "grub." Either they work a portion of the year to earn money enough to "grub-stake" themselves out of their savings, or else they enthuse some one into a belief that they will find a mine; and the man who finds the grub-stake is entitled to a one-half interest in any mining property which the prospector may locate. A grub-stake is a term used to designate the provisions carried by the prospector or the sleuth in search of gold. These necessarily are very limited, as he has to carry them on his back; a robe of fox-skin, in which to sleep, as being the warmest fur procurable; flour, bacon, salt, sugar and tea. The only cooking-utensils are a frying-pan, tin plate, tin cup, knife and fork, pick and shovel and gold-pan.

Birch-bark is in profusion everywhere, and peeling it from the nearest tree the prospector builds a fire and cooks his flour, salt and water in a cake as thin as a flap-jack, and the frying of his bacon greases the pan for this elaborate meal.

At the Christmas holidays of 1897 and 1898 the exodus of Eastern people to the Klondike reached its height.

The farmer left his plow in the furrow, the mechanic laid down his tools, the professional man, least fitted of all for the struggle, closed his office, and turned their faces to the frozen fields of that great northwest territory in Canada and Alaska. The newspapers devoted columns to the exploiting of the new gold-fields.

Few alone remember the prophetic words of William H. Seward when, having completed the negotiations for the purchase of Alaska from the Russian government, which was then considered a political movement for territorial aggrandization, he said, "The generation which shall come after us will recognize that we have left them an inheritance more rich and more desirable than Australia or India is to Great Britain."

"Pike's Peak or bust" was the cry when Colorado began to yield her golden store, but that was in the heart of the Continent and the way direct and the distance and dangers a purely comparative quantity.

But Alaska meant a land of eternal snow and ice, the crossing of the continent, a voyage north nearly to the pole, and all the appalling terrors of the unknown and probably the unknowable.

But the lust of gold is an unquenchable passion.

# CHAPTER I

I HAD been in the practice of medicine in Chicago, Ill., U. S. A., for a number of years, and for the three years preceding the "find" on the Klondike, had been closely confined by hospital-work in an official position. I had decided to take a rest. But where? I had traveled extensively and had no special desire to revisit any of the places I had been, and for some days was in a quandary just what to do. One morning my secretary came in before I had arisen, and playfully pointed out a long article in the morning paper on the Klondike, and said:

"Why don't you go there? It will be quite new, and you can practice anywhere and perhaps get a mine and make a fortune."

My resolution was taken on the instant, and I said: "Yes, I *will* go to the Klondike. I *will* attend the sick, and I *will* make a fortune." And that is why I went to the gold-fields and how this story came to be written.

In January, 1898, having some business in Portland, Ore., I took the train over the Northern Pacific bound for that city. My baggage was not bulky, a sealskin coat and hat being the most important items in my outfit.

The other requisites, I was advised, I could provide myself with to better advantage on the coast. Having finished my professional work in Portland, I took a train for San Francisco. The reason for this apparent getting away from my route was very simple, for at that point I could get better accommodations on better steamers than from a more northern port. Arrived in San Francisco and found the conditions were little if any better. Thousands of men were there waiting for steamship accommodations to the northward. For the third time in its history San Francisco had gone "gold-mad." The days of " '49," when the city was one of canvas, and the people came over the plains across the Isthmus of Panama and through the Straits of Magellan to the new Eldorado, were being re-enacted in a city of palaces instead of one of canvas tents.

The days of Big Bonanza were not more full of excitement than those which followed the reports of the richness and extent of the great strike upon the Klondike. People, principally men, came into the city on every railway train and in wagon trains, and the old-time miners who came on foot were not lacking; and, as in all times of mining excitement, the crowd was a motley one. They made up parties among themselves to stick together and bunk together while going into the Yukon Territory and Alaska, and made common cause in their adventure. I was fortunate in not having to wait long in the city by the Golden Gate.

A friend had given me a strong letter of introduction to a relative who was going in to construct a telephone-line in company with three other gentlemen. This was a most fortunate incident. They invited me to join their party, which I did.

They were cultivated gentlemen, and saved me from much that was disagreeable which I would have encountered had I been thrown with the rougher element.

They took my passage to Dyea, the point of debarkation, the cost being much less than was to have been expected in view of the prices charged in past periods of mining excitement. I paid fifteen dollars from San Francisco to Victoria, and sixty-five dollars from Victoria to Dyea. This included one hundred pounds of baggage and a bunk, or berth—as you may call it. The latter were put up in every available inch of space, and when we packed ourselves into them we were as snug as though encased in the Catacombs of Paris. ?

The food was passable at first. The meat was killed on board, and we had plenty of canned provisions, but the number of passengers far excelled the capacity of the kitchen and store-rooms, so that as the days went by we were on shorter and shorter rations and the food was of less desirable quality.

We left San Francisco on the steamship Umatilla February 5, and went into the port of Victoria, B. C., two days later.

At Victoria the first serious work of the journey was undertaken. After leaving here we were beyond the pale of civilization. From here we passed into the great Northwest, and the road led to the new mining-camp amid the frozen zone where Nature had hidden her treasure.

It is a curious but a historical fact that either in the frozen North or pestiferous tropical swamps Nature hides her stores of gold to lure men to seek at the risk of their lives.

At Victoria, B. C., we were compelled to outfit for the journey and the trip across Chilcoot Pass. As many adventurous spirits richer in hope and pluck than money had hit the trail without a sufficient supply of provisions and had suffered hardships and death before reaching the other side, the authorities interfered and prescribed the rations.

The requisite amount of food prescribed by the authorities to obviate this condition of affairs was not less than six hundred pounds to each person.

This consisted usually of flour, bacon, beans, canned tomatoes, sugar, tea, rice and salt—not a very epicurean menu, but nourishing and kept within the weight.

After a day's shopping the results were amusing, had it not been indicative of perhaps fatal troubles for the people who were going where they knew not and after spoils they would never acquire. The scenes on the pier were certainly novel, not to say picturesque. Especially was this true of the Swedes and Norwegians, far, far from their native friends. The favorite costume of these brave empire-builders seemed to be a suit of bright yellow felted cloth, about half an inch in thickness, riveted together; a fur cap of cone-shape, which could be pulled down over the face, the "windows" of the soul peering out through panes of isinglass. Tons of provisions and clothing, other tons of miner's tools, the flickering light of great torches making grotesque shadows on the wharf, this motley crowd of people of varied nations moving restlessly about, and if you have an imagination you can conjure up a picture the like of which will never be seen again.

These tools, stores and provisions were bonded by the customs authorities through the United States Territory to Lake Bennett in British Columbia; so that we had the benefit of the lower prices without paying duty. Many, however, were not aware of this method of evading duty, outfitted in the United States, and had endless trials and tribulations with both the Canadian and American customs officers. And the blackmail which was levied on these innocents was a wonder, and both Canadian and American revenue officers were equally culpable and dishonest.

We had purchased our tickets at Victoria on the American steamer Seattle, but the British customs officer ordered us ashore, saying she was overloaded by one hundred tons, and had more than the licensed number of passengers.

To plead, to swear, to rave was of no avail, and ashore we had to go. The next ship booked to sail north was the Clara Nevada, and the first one to come south, with not only the news of the miners, but with a cargo of gold-dust and nuggets in proof of the stories told of the wealth in sight on the Yukon. On her were the old and experienced miners who brought their dust with them, the proceeds of the first wash-up of importance which took place in the Klondike. It was expected that the Clara Nevada would sail in three days after we landed, but she did not appear that day nor the following one. There were people waiting for friends they had not seen in several years—the mothers, wives and sweethearts of the returning miners. The streets and the wharf were filled with a constantly increasing crowd. One old character, a sailor nicknamed "Black Jack," shook his head ominously. He ran out to sea in his little sloop and scanned the horizon several times a day, but there was no sign of the Clara Nevada. The steamer due was watched for with impatience. The crowd of waiting people increased daily. The pier was always alive with men straining their eyes like a castaway on the desert.

The thought always in every man's mind was, "The man ahead of me may get the claim that should be mine."

So day after day passed. Then a ship was sighted, and a mighty shout went up. The Clara Nevada was booked to sail for the gold-fields February 14. She had arrived at last. But the old sailor shook his head sadly and said, "That's not the Clara Nevada." As she approached the anchorage she was seen to be the Islander, and brought the sad news that she had seen the Clara Nevada's topmast sticking out above the water between Skagway and Juno. The ship had sunk with all on board and with her load of treasure; not one person survived to tell the story. The crew and sixty-eight passengers were lost. The purser was a young man fond of adventure, of good family, and his mother offered a reward of fifty thousand dollars for the recovery of his body. A short time after some Indians fishing not far from where the ship went down found the body, which had washed ashore with the ice and rested upon the ice gathered along the shore. The body was dressed as usual in these latitudes— in a full set of furs, showing clearly that he had gone to his death in the performance of his duty and died at his post.

Conjecture was rife as to how and why the ship was lost. The only evidence was found by his body, for the mustache and hair were singed to an extent that showed clearly that the ship had been destroyed by fire, and under such circumstances in that latitude escape is almost impossible.

Those who jump overboard, even with life-preservers, perish with the cold in a short time, or are sucked under when the burning ship sinks and makes a whirlpool of her own, while those who remain on the ship are lost as soon as the flames reach the water's edge.

The steamship Islander coming back on her regular trip offered the opportunity which for ten days we had waited with much impatience to get away to the frozen North. The desire to get into the gold-fields is as strong a passion as the human animal is capable of, and each day's delay was most irritating, and each day longer than its predecessor. Our outfits were ready for embarkation; we had, especially the women, less than a dozen in all, no source of amusement or recreation; men could gamble, and did, to pass away the time, but we women could only talk and dream of the golden harvest for which we had abandoned the comforts and luxuries of our Eastern homes. But no one was discouraged. It was a bond of interest which bound us together, whether a lady physician, like myself, or a girl going into a dance-hall.

We were all thousands of miles away from home. A new life confronted us, and the spirit of helpfulness pervaded the waiting assemblage.

Sleep was out of the question. The rattle of the hoisting-machinery, the cries of the stevedores and the hoarsely shouted orders of the officers all contributed to make a veritable pandemonium which was illuminated by the fitful glare of the torches which served to light the work, and to make the rest of the land and sea blacker and blacker and to fresco the wharf and ship with Rembrandtesque shadows.

Day was fast breaking in the east and the sun rising out of the bosom of the Pacific Ocean when the work of stowing the cargo was complete and the order given for the passengers to embark.

The Islander was an English vessel, iron propeller, built in Glasgow about eight years before for service in the Alaskan waters. She was brought around the Horn to Victoria, B. C. The license permitted of her carrying only three hundred passengers, but when there is gold in sight and gold coming out of the North, officials are not always too particular as to the counting of noses. On the trip of which I am writing we carried six hundred and eighty-four passengers, and as nearly every person had a dog, and some a dozen, the latter became a very distinct factor in the problem of transportation. Their provision was to me a problem. I found, however, that the dogs would eat a special coarse variety of dried salmon known as "dog-salmon," and which is put up in bales like hay and thence fed to the dogs—not a diet which would tempt the appetite; and yet the native dog will do an average of forty-five miles a day and a special breed of them will put sixty-five miles behind them in twenty-four hours. So you can see that the dog, while always man's best friend, is particularly so in the frozen North.

In addition we had sixty oxen and a hundred head of horses for drawing heavy loads from Dyea to Sheep Camp. These animals were a most valuable adjunct, since the dogs are of little use when the grade is steep, as it is on this part of the trail. Once over the Chilcoot Pass the dogs begin to do their work, and along the lakes and rivers a team will draw loads averaging five hundred pounds, four dogs constituting a team.

We had also about one hundred tons of provisions, eight hundred tons of baggage and nine hundred tons of freight. This comprised all the necessities of the miners, dog-sleds, picks, shovels, axes, gold-pans and snow-shoes. A gold-pan is used by the prospector to wash the dirt out of the gold. It is a primitive contrivance, much the same shape as an ordinary wash-basin. It has been in use many years. The miners put a shovelful of dirt into the pan and immerse it in a pool or tub of water. They keep shaking it all the time; the water washes away first the dirt, and then the gravel, and finally there is left nothing but the gold-dust and nuggets, which having the highest specific gravity remain at the bottom of the pan.

## CHAPTER II

EARLY on the morning of February 17 hundreds of people assembled on the pier, relatives and friends of those who were starting for the gold-fields. Some of them came hundreds of miles from the interior, and strong men wept bitterly as they bade farewell to their loved ones so soon to drop below the horizon and whose return was most uncertain from an expedition so befraught with dangers and difficulties. Many of those who bade a tearful farewell to their loved ones never heard of them thereafter. They dropped out of sight and were lost to the world. Their fate is and will always remain a mystery.

The Islander cast off her lines and put to sea at 7.30 and sailed out into the sun track under the command of Captain John Irving, who shortly turned her nose to the northwest. She had a full cargo destined for those who had already entered upon their life in the mines of the Yukon Territory of Canada and Alaska. We had traveled about four thousand miles, eaten and drunk when and where we could, and at last were embarked on the final stage of our journey. The dogs seemed to have a premonition of the fate that awaited them and sent up their protest to heaven against the cruelty of mankind. If they had really known they were to meet with the cruel treatment which I afterward saw some of them receive they would all have jumped overboard, as a few of them did soon after we got under way. The old-time superstition of a dog howling at the approach of death in a neighborhood seemed to take possession of the passengers and each looked at the other in the most abject terror, but it was a terror which begot silence and discouraged speech. We had a voyage of eleven days before us, perhaps one less or one more, as the weather permitted. Our cramped accommodations and our rather limited diet did not serve to dampen the enthusiasm of the gold-seekers.

It would fill a volume to describe the motley crowd of passengers. The most interesting were the old-time prospectors and miners long past middle age, their skins tanned by years of exposure to the color and consistency of leather and this drawn over a rawboned frame, lean and muscular and devoid of an ounce of superfluous flesh. As for the rest they were tenderfeet making their first venture into a wild country. College professors, bankrupt merchants, bank clerks, lawyers and business men of all kinds made up the remainder.

Naturally the old-timers were the center of attraction. They did not hesitate to draw the "long bow" in their reminiscences of the days of " '49," of which they possessed all the traditions; of the days of the big Bonanza Mine in California, when Marcus, Flood and O'Brien were the mining kings; of Senator Stewart's big silver strike; of the terrors of Death Valley, and of the luck of Senator "Bill" Clark. To the imagination of these neophytes embarking on their first adventures this was like pouring oil on the flames. They talked of gold all day and dreamed of it all night.

Among the few women on board was a petite young Englishwoman who had her innings each day by telling us what they did "at home." Her husband, to whom she alluded affectionately at all times as "Jim dear," was a fine specimen of the British type who belong to the remittance class.

"She felt vexed, in fact, she was a trifle angry, you know." She sat up all night that she might be at the head of the procession and secure the very best berth to be had on the vessel, and spent the remainder of the day in boasting to her less fortunate fellow passengers. Her stateroom, which was the largest on the ship, "you know," had double berths, "you know," and the door opened into the social hall, "you know," and the window opened from the inside so "Jim dear" could sit so comfortably by himself in his own stateroom and amuse himself, "you know, watching the seals play hooky." And the stationary bowl was quite large enough, "you know," to afford a b-a-u-t-h, "you know." Their tickets being first-class entitled them to a seat at the captain's table, "you know." She was so glad she had staid up all night and secured such excellent accommodations. She felt so sorry, "you know," for others less fortunate. As for herself she could endure hardships rather gracefully, "you know." She had ridden horseback over the mountains of

South Africa and heard the panthers cry at midnight, and saw something once about half a mile away on the side of the mountain that looked like a bear, but Jim dear had never had to undergo hardships in all his dear life and it was for him she was most concerned on the trip, "you know." You can easily imagine her dismay and surprise when she boarded the ship and found that during the night they had utilized every inch of space on the inside of that vessel. It was occupied by tiers and tiers of the most rudely constructed berths. Social halls, ladies' cabins, salons were all turned into a "bunk house." The large stateroom she had so carefully chosen for Jim dear's comfort now had four berths instead of two. The stationary bowl had been removed. The view from the large window was entirely obstructed by crates and crates of nasty dogs of the most ordinary breeding, "you know."

"Oh!" she cried, "this is terrible—abominable—really disgraceful, you know. I must see the captain at once. Jim dear and I have first-class tickets and I shall insist on having the very best accommodations procurable on this ship, you know."

It was growing cold. Those who had remained out on the deck caring for their dogs dropped in one after another till the air became so stifling one could scarcely breathe. Doors had to be left open the entire time regardless of the extreme cold. Yet everybody was good-natured and jolly.

The sea became choppy after a few hours and

nearly every one was seasick. We had no trouble serving meals for two days. Then everybody wanted to eat. When their appetites returned then the trouble began. Everybody wanted to eat and to eat at the same time. The appetite which succeeds seasickness and the salt air combined made them all ravenous. No seats were assigned to the passengers; it was purely a case of first come first served. It grew worse and worse from day to day—that mad rush for food. Finally they began to drop down over the railing into the main dining cabin below. Those who had formed in line and were waiting to get down the steps into the dining saloon found the tables already occupied by those who had, as it were, "just dropped in."

This naturally bred trouble, and one day the steward drew a revolver. In a second a hundred guns were out, and it looked like a real case of "rough house," or rather of "rough ship." But Captain Irving was promptly on the scene, and so diplomatic and tactful did he prove that things quieted down promptly, and his arrangement of the meal hours gave perfect satisfaction thereafter.

The next few days were devoid of incident except that it was stormy. We ran into a gale of wind about three hundred miles north of Victoria and took refuge in Safety Cove, near Point Alexander. The gale raged with such force that it became prudent to seek this refuge at once. The wind whistled through the standing rigging and howled about the hull, causing the ship to pitch violently until we had made a change of course and stood in for Safety Cove.

This is a small body of water which will not shelter more than two vessels at one time. The sheltering of the cove from the wind and waves raging outside gave us the first rest we had enjoyed for days. In shape it is a horse-shoe lagoon, and as we steamed into it the moment we had passed through the narrow inlet which gave ingress to the cove—a marvel to those on board—we ran into water as placid as a summer lake in the East.

The mountains surrounding the cove rose almost perpendicular from the water's edge to a great height. The dark green foliage of the spruce trees, some of them two hundred feet in height, covered the mountain sides and softened the outlines of the forest.

This great forest cast a myriad of shadows' reflections over the diminutive bay until it seemed with the still waters that we were floating upon a sea of foliage.

We had barely anchored in Safety Cove when our supply of water gave out. This was the most trying of our experiences on shipboard. Thirst exaggerates itself at sea as it does in the desert. The women wept, men cursed and prayed in many different languages. A few went gunning for the captain. Our good captain assured us that at daylight we would try to cross Queen Charlotte's Sound and take a full supply of water at the Indian village called Bella Bella, a distance of forty miles across the sound. All the wet goods on board were turned over that night by the captain to the passengers and crew. Surrounded by ice and snow we suffered the tortures of Tantalus. Soda water, beer and wine were exhausted, until at last in sheer desperation men drank catsup and Worcestershire sauce from the bottle.

All this time the hundreds of dogs on board suffering for water kept up the most unearthly howling and yelping and were answered in terrorizing screams from the wild animals in the mountains just over our heads.

We were not consoled by the recital of the history of the cove. A whaling vessel had been captured in this cove only a few years before and every one of the crew murdered. She was a whaler starting out for a three years' voyage and was heavily provisioned. She took refuge from storm in Safety Cove where we were then lying. All on board were sleeping peacefully when a few Indians of the Bella Bella tribe sneaked on them at night (in their little skin kayaks), and massacred every one of them. The object of the attack was to loot the ship, which they did and abandoned her to her fate.

It stormed all night and the lightning was both terrific and beautiful. Some of the foreigners, who were very superstitious, hid in their bunks, covered up their heads and shivered with fright. Even one American was decidedly inconsolable. It is the unknown that is always terrifying.

All night the sighing of the wind through the branches of the huge pines sang a requiem for the murdered dead. The underbrush was covered with ice and snow and the conglomerate mass assumed the most grotesque figures. As they caught and reflected the lightning, they looked like corpses—and to add to the fright of the already panic-stricken passengers, many proclaimed them the ghosts of the murdered crew.

## CHAPTER III

WHEN morning dawned we started to cross Queen Charlotte's Sound, a distance of some forty miles. Although the Safety Cove's huge, rocky wall had sheltered us, when we put to sea no sooner had we rounded the point than the gale struck the Islander with terrific force. The captain saw at once it was impossible to cross the sound and the only thing to do was to put back into Safety Cove. But that was more easily said than done with that gale and sea running in Queen Charlotte's Sound.

By good seamanship he put her about, but when she was broadside on the tremendous seas she keeled over on her side, and it seemed as though it was all up with us. Passengers were thrown from their bunks through glass doors, cut and bruised. All the dogs and freight on the upper deck went overboard, nearly every dish in the pantry was broken, horses and oxen killed and crippled. She then righted herself and made her way back into Safety Cove, where religious services were held and all the passengers joined in singing the praises of our Redeemer. The passengers, who had been impatient to get out of Safety Cove that morning, were on their knees praying in a dozen different languages while she was on her side. They expected to be lost.

Finally it began to snow. Snow-water does not quench thirst but we cooled our parched lips and tongues and used it as sparingly as possible to relieve the acuteness of our sufferings.

At ten o'clock the next morning the gale had abated and we steamed out into Queen Charlotte's Sound and at one o'clock we sighted Bella Bella. A shout of joy went up from every one on board at the certainty of soon getting plenty of fresh water.

Bella Bella is an Indian village whose early days are shrouded in antiquity, but their traditions carry the village back long before the time of Christopher Columbus. Here we got a plentiful supply of pure water from a natural artesian flowing well and satisfied the craving of our palates for "aqua pura."

The result of our exposure to this storm and the eating of snow put almost every one of the passengers on the sick list. There were twenty-six cases of pneumonia and eighteen cases of acute pleurisy.

We arrived at Wrangel's on Wednesday, February 23. This proved to be a village of from 150 to 200 log-cabins and tents and a population of about five hundred persons. There was a court-house there which reminded me of the log pig-pens that the darkies erected down in old Virginia.

A passenger was arrested and dragged before the judge for the purpose of extorting some whiskey which he had with him for medicinal purposes and which the judge and sheriff thought would be a pleasant lubricant for their interior economy. He was an innocent-looking chap with a smile that was child-like and bland—but they had made a mistake. He was a Montana cowboy and he whipped out a couple of "44" guns, began shooting with both hands, cleaned out the court-house in a minute, and that court never sat again.

The professional element was well represented by eight lawyers, two doctors and two drug-stores. The remainder of the population were engaged in canning salmon for the use of the world.

Here was our first opportunity to set foot on shore since we started, and all hands took advantage of it gleefully, the more so when they discovered that there were a large number of eating places. A descent was made upon these, ship's fare having become tiresome. The stopping of ships there readily explained what at first glance seemed a phantom of restaurants.

After a few hours we continued on our way northward and on Thursday and in a little over 24 hours we reached Juno Alaska. On the trip we stopped at a distress signal displayed by a vessel high and dry on the rocks. No one was on board. We found her to be the Corona and a vessel which preceded us had taken off her passengers and crew and they were already on their way to the gold fields. She was in a narrow channel off shore and went at full speed on the rocks. So great was the impact that her bow was driven 20 feet into the air and she was left there immovable.

Juno Alaska is a town of some 4,000 inhabitants. It is near the great Treadwell mines. It is a typical town of the mining camps. The town was running wide open day and night. Dance halls and gambling houses furnished the diversion of the miners and shopkeepers.

On the corner of one of the prominent streets I recognized the voice of "The nice young American," who had entertained us on the voyage with religious songs. He had erected a platform of drygoods boxes and enterprisingly started the old envelope game. I stopped and this is what I heard:

"Here it is, gentlemen; $3.00 to you, sir. Now who will be the next? I will be kind enough to offer you another. Who will take this chance for a half-dollar and take whatever it calls for? It is too bad this one is worth nothing. You must try again."

After a few hours here we steamed north to Skagway, reaching there Friday night, February 28. The thermometer was 23 degrees below zero and our ship was a mass of ice—sides, deck and rigging. We were all put ashore at Skagway though our tickets read to Dyea. They could not land in Dyea, so the officers said.

The customs officers were there. All the goods were unloaded at Skagway. We had to pay 25 cents a day for wharf privileges for each bag or box unloaded. Then we must pay $5.00 a ton for freighting by tugboat to Dyea, and pay two fares. You had to put up money at Skagway for duties or pay a broker twenty dollars for making out custom house papers; then the officers would send a convoy with you at a cost of six dollars a day and board to see that you didn't open the goods in the United States if they were English or Canadian goods. If you bought your outfit in Victoria as we did you would wish you had outfitted in the United States before you got through with the United States customs officers at Skagway. And if you outfitted in the United States in Seattle you would have to pay as much as the goods cost you before you got through with the Canadian customs officers on top of Chilcoot Pass. It was a case, so far as the pilgrim was concerned, of pull Dick, pull Devil. Incessantly the pilgrim got the worst of it. It is a disgrace to civilization to see such blackmail covered up with the American eagle and the English crown of King George. Many a man who could not stand the graft after packing his outfit to the top of the Chilcoot Pass sacrificed his outfit and returned; others packed on their backs over the summit till they had satisfied the Shylocks with the pound of flesh.

An American customs officer took from a sick patient of mine suffering from acute pleurisy a bottle of whiskey which I had begged from a passenger on board ship, and because he did not want to give it up was threatened with arrest. Yet in Skagway you could buy all the whiskey you wanted for a dollar a drink and one saloon was supplied daily by the customs officers. The duty on a horse was $30, on a dog $7.50.

## CHAPTER IV

OUR party went on to Dyea. I shall never forget that night in Dyea. After sleeping on a board floor in a log cabin with only my fox robe wrapped around me and my traveling bag for a pillow we arose with the sun and made preparations for that part of the journey that every one so much dreaded. It was 23 degrees below zero that night.

We were at the end of our steamship journey and must "hit" the trail. We started in company with about a thousand others up that narrow, winding canyon. Its almost perpendicular walls were covered with glaciers. The snow was 20 feet deep in places. A hard trail about two feet wide wound around abrupt bluffs for twenty miles up the canyon to the foot of Chilcoot Pass. It was my first experience of rough life and it held a certain amount of charm of novelty. All day long we tramped through snow and ice. As night overtook us we made camp under the overhanging rocks along the side of the mountain. When we had eaten a cold lunch I requested that my bed be arranged that I might lie down for the night. I had "hoofed it," as the miners say, for ten miles and was very tired. A hole was shoveled in the snow just under the projection of a large bowlder. A few spruce boughs were carefully arranged and I folded my fox robe around me and lay down within a few feet of the four California gentlemen whom I had met and traveled with from San Francisco, they agreeing to give me their protection for my professional services if needed on the trail.

A fire was kept burning all night as the mountains through that part were filled with wild animals that could be heard near us during the night. I had scarcely touched my rude bed before I was sound asleep and awoke early in the morning refreshed and ready for the day's journey. We reached Sheep Camp that night and there we pitched our tents and had every comfort that camp life can give in that country. There we found at the foot of that mammoth formation of rocks called Chilcoot Pass a city of tents, about 200 in all. In less than a week it had increased to several thousand. The trail was blocked as far down the canyon as the eye could carry. People and provisions continued to arrive day and night for six weeks until there was scarcely room to pitch another tent.

From Sheep Camp to the foot of Chilcoot Pass was about four miles. The grade became very steep. The provisions and freight had to be all landed on top of this mountain peak. About half-way to the top it was possible to use horses and oxen and dogs. From that point to the top men had to pack their belongings on their backs. The trail was only about two feet wide and was packed snow a dozen feet deep. On either side the snow was loose and if a man slipped off the trail with his load he disappeared never to be seen again.

Ascending Chilkoot Pass, Spring of 1898.

On the left-hand side of the trail was an immense glacier from which a section broke loose and plunged down the mountain side all the way into Sheep Camp. Several people living in tents lost their lives at this time. These facts will demonstrate to the friends of men who started for the gold-fields why they were never heard of again. Mail service was almost a nullity and each one was too busy taking care of himself and his own life to bother writing to friends and relatives. Those who perished in the snow left no signs as to who they were or whence they came. Nicknames were the common identifications and as in all new mining camps such titles as "Swift Water Bill," "Black Sullivan," "Duke of Scookum," "Caribou Billy" and "Easy Money" are fair samples of the nomenclature of the Klondike.

In climbing the Chilcoot Pass we started from a point on the side of the mountain about three-fourths of a mile to the peak of the summit, a trail which led up so steep a declivity that steps had been cut into the frozen snow and ice with an axe, and ropes stretched down the sides to assist the travelers up the ascent, which was nearly perpendicular. The miners followed each other closely, the one behind putting his foot down in the footprints of the man ahead of him.

Viewed from a point below the procession resembled nothing so much as a procession of black ants. A few days later there was a snowslide from this mountain and the entire trail was engulfed in the avalanche for two miles down the canyon. The snow was a hundred feet deep in places. How many lives were lost will never be known, for while the sea gives up its dead the snow and ice preserves and keeps its bodies awaiting the last trump.

We started from Sheep Camp at daybreak and reached the summit at noonday. I was just one hour climbing the last three-quarters of a mile to the top of the Chilcoot Pass. The horses and oxen and dogs were sent through White Pass from Skagway to Lake Linderman, a much greater distance but more accessible. Just over the peak on top of the mountain we found the Canadian customs officials. As our goods were purchased in Victoria we had no such trouble as did those who came in with American goods. The freight being loaded on sleds on top of the mountain it was coasted down for a mile and a half to the foot of the Chilcoot Pass on the opposite side. Only one sled was started at a time and it was followed by its owner in the primitive fashion of country schoolboys who sit down on the frozen surface and slide to the foot of the mountain, which brought him to the ice in Long Lake. At this point we found our dogs, and both men and dogs joined in pulling the sleds on a gentle incline to Caribou Crossing. The first place we struck was Lake Linderman, where we staid and slept one night. Thence we continued to Caribou Crossing where we were among the first to make camp. When we had reached Lake Linderman I became very weary and gladly met a man whose necessity compelled him to sell a fine dog, a young St. Bernard called Prince Napoleon. He was of enormous size and great strength though not a year old. His hair was silky and a light lemon color with a white collar around his neck. His tail was long and beautifully feathered and he had all the courage and intelligence of his race. I then purchased a willow basket sled and a set of harness and settled myself down to the first comfort I had had on the trail. He would frisk around mornings and seemed pleased to be put in the harness. He soon attached himself to me and slept at my feet every night.

In the basket sled with me was my fox robe and my dressing bag and flying light. We traveled day after day until we reached Caribou Crossing, where we were to remain and wait for the ice to break up and go out of the lakes and rivers, and where the men after looking about took our party up the Watson river about three miles, just across Lake Bennett from Caribou Crossing. At this place timber of the largest and finest quality was plentiful and the men found good exercise whipsawing lumber for building the boats to take us on to the gold-fields as soon as the ice went out of the rivers. Here we enjoyed restful nights after the trials of the steamship voyage and the hardships and perils of the Chilcoot Pass. It occupied the six weeks we were camped here before the ice went out. Our party had escaped accident and sickness up to this time, more fortunate than most in this respect.

One day when the boat-building had begun

one of the party, whom we called Mr. Cady, fell from the sawhorse, being in his opinion badly injured. He was a good fellow but was unfortunately born tired. He had a quaint turn of humor and explained his accident to me in this wise.

"Well, you see the trouble was that I had one more bean on the left side of my stomach than I had on the right side, so I very naturally lost my balance and tumbled to the ground."

Cady was the agent of the Sunset Telephone Co., going in with his assistants. A young man very blond and an expert in his own business, he did not take kindly to anything more in the line of hard work than to tumble off the sawhorse, and leave the boat-building job to others. He was so long and thin and bald-headed that he was known on the trail as the "Kangaroo." Always smiling and joking, he was the life of the party and the laughs he evoked by his witticisms served to help over many rough places on our journey.

Walter, another of the party, was a big, husky fellow, well educated, with a bazoo like a steam calliope. He had been a politician and when his voice was commented upon he said he was the son of his father, who was very religious, and when he prayed could be heard a mile.

Richard was a German and a citizen of the "Vaterland." He was one of the most enthusiastic admirers of Bismarck, the "Iron Chancellor," to whose utterances he always referred as being law.

George was the good boy of the party and as loyal to King Edward as Richard was to Bis-

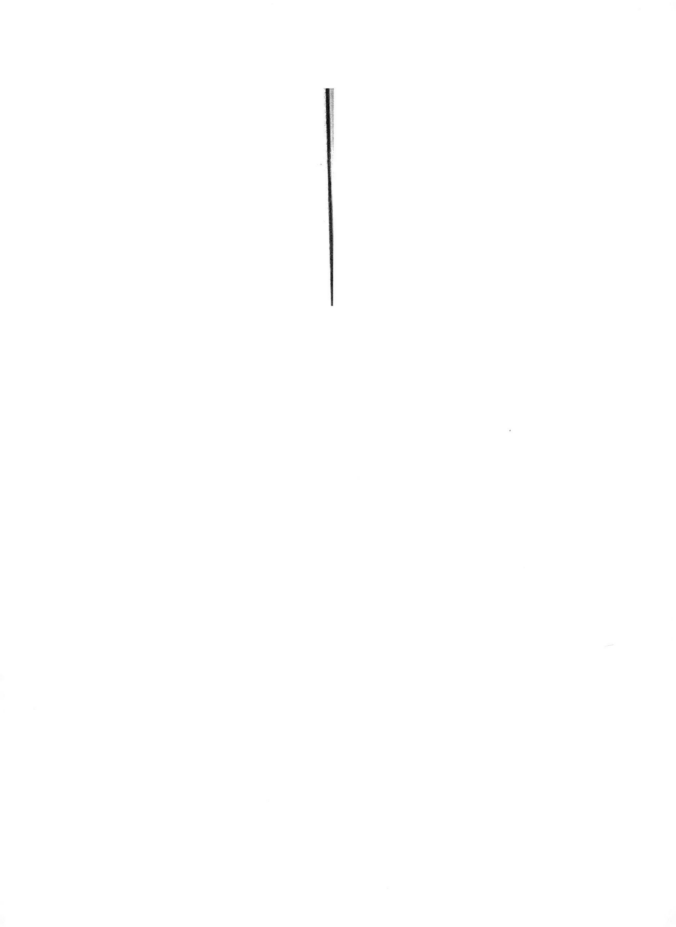

marck. One day at the dinner-table he said he would never become a citizen of the United States, where he had lived most of his life. On my request for a reason for this declaration he said, "Because the United States does not protect her citizens in foreign countries."

I replied that she did protect her citizens.

"How patriotic and charming of you," he said in his smiling way. "But now just tell me where your government has protected her citizens here in Alaska. They certainly did not stand by Mr. Ivey in Skagway and he was in the right, when he took the law in his own hands. After Joaquin Miller's brother shot down the British flag Ivey served official notice upon the Canadian customs officers to take bags and baggage and 'hike' themselves over the Chilcoot Pass within 24 hours."

"Well," I said, "didn't they 'hike over'?" And he replied, "Did not your government remove Mr. Ivey shortly thereafter? Whereas, if an English officer had done the same thing he would have been sent to Parliament."

Walter cited at once the Venezuelan incident during President Cleveland's administration and other similar episodes.

"Ah!" said George, "but the individual rarely gets protection." The conversation was waxing hot when I tied my handkerchief to my pencil and stuck it in the beanpot which was sitting in the middle of the table. Amid the laugh that followed this raising of the flag of truce the incident was forgotten.

## CHAPTER V

THE boats were completed and we held a council of war. The ice had gone out of the Watson river, a narrow canyon stream, but had not gone out of Lake Bennett, so we took our boats and went down to the lake where we put them on the ice and hauled them on sleds to Caribou Crossing where we made camp again, awaiting with the constantly increasing crowd, the opening of navigation. My companions thought it advisable to send me in a small boat, called a peterboro canoe, in charge of Fred Eversole, of Seattle, a most expert oarsman. He advised against taking my dog in the same boat. "Said and I agreed with him" that he would follow along the banks near which we would voyage.

We had hardly started when we got into a whirlpool and the boat capsized in 20 feet of water. I knew I could not swim. I knew my feet touched bottom. I felt it, and then I came to the surface half drowned and strangling. The oarsman clung to the overturned boat which drifted rapidly down the swift stream and stranded on a sandbar about six hundred feet below. As I disappeared beneath the water I heard a most pitiful cry, followed by the sound of a large body dropping from a high place into the water. When I came up my dog Napoleon was swimming about the place where I had disappeared. He seized me and I grappled him convulsively. Instantly I saw I was drowning the dog as well as myself and I let go and took hold of his long hair and he towed me about 200 feet down the stream where he saw a safe landing and dragged me on shore. I was benumbed with cold. The water was like ice-water. I was almost insensible for a while. When I could open my eyes my faithful dog was standing over me wagging his tail with a most mournful expression. Some men had hastened to my assistance who were boat-building near by and saw us capsize, but Napoleon's growls and display of teeth drove them away. Shortly I was able to get on my feet and was taken to a cabin and got a change of dry clothes and some hot coffee. Then I and my noble dog started and walked down the banks of the river to Lake Bennett where we met the boatman. There we found the solid ice and walked side by side, "me and my dog," across Lake Bennett to Caribou Crossing.

While we were boat-building on the shores of Watson River the population of Caribou Crossing had increased from a few hundred to some 12,000 souls. These people were all bound for the gold-fields and this being only a waiting-place prior to embarkation there was none of the gambling and drinking usual in camps where gold is being taken out.

The enterprise of modern or yellow journalism was never better illustrated than at Caribou

Crossing, when a printer named Swinehart, from some Canadian town, had set up on the ice, under canvas, a hand-press and font of type. It was newsy and whatever news came into camp was handed him by the recipients of letters and so the whole company had the benefit of the various items of impersonal gossip from the East. I bought the first copy and stood by the press and saw it come off, paying 25 cents for it. This being the first paper published in the Yukon, the editor, proprietor, compositor and proof-reader took my quarter, the first he received, and set it in a mortise in the feed-bed of the press.

The relief from the strain of the past weeks naturally caused a reaction and fun and frolic held sway among the gold-seekers. The ice was evidently getting ready to move out and we were all on the watch day and night. It had loosened around the edges and the great cracks began to spread across the surface in an imitation of a spider's web. To pass away the time, which we still had to wait, and during which we all became more and more impatient, one of our fellow voyagers, a Mr. White, a real "Southern gentleman" prominent in the politics of his state and who was accompanying his son, a young man on his first prospecting tour, gave a unique dinner.

They were both men of extraordinary stature and physique, and probably the two finest specimens of educated physical manhood I saw in that country. The dinner was given in his tent and the invitations were written on shavings from the boat-builders' work.

They read as follows:

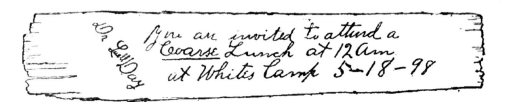

The menu was as primitive as the cards of invitation, but one does not have to take bitters to get up an appetite on the trail. We had corn bread, beans and bacon, rice pudding and coffee, a veritable feast.

Our enjoyment was great, especially as our host told darky stories by the score with inimitable dialect. He related a story of a young nigger who went into a store and asked for a good razor.

The salesman looked over a lot and selecting one handed it out with the remark: "There's as good a razor as any man ever shaved with."

"Shaved wif! Shaved wif! I doan want no razzer to shave wif, I want one for social purposes, sir."

At daybreak on the second of June, while the camp was wrapped in slumber, a sudden and peculiar noise awoke us all. It was a crackling and grinding noise which proclaimed the fact that the ice had at last broken up and was going out, piling itself one cake upon another (some of which were eight feet in thickness and twenty feet square) in its mad rush hurried forward by the swift mountain current toward the Behring Sea.

About ten o'clock in the morning the lake had

cleared so that the boats which were already loaded were able to follow the ice down the river. Every man was anxious to get his boat in the water and get away first. Yet there was no fouling or colliding. The whip-sawing of the lumber for those boats had cost far too much labor and time for them to be jeopardized recklessly.

We drifted with the current six miles to Lake Tagish, where were the barracks of the Northwest Mounted Police. Here we had to have our boats numbered and register the names of the passengers in case of their being lost. It cost a small compusory fee, about one dollar.

At Lake Tagish I met a Mr. and Mrs. Wilson and the latter's brother, Fred Baker, from the life-saving station at San Francisco. I had treated Mr. Wilson at Lake Linderman. He had pneumonia and since that time I had not seen them until now. He had suffered a relapse. I left my party with whom I was able to keep in touch with their full consent, knowing the necessity of the case.

Young Baker in a single scow and the whole camp outfit preceded us down the river. He selected the camping ground and hung out the flag to call us in shore, where we would find a fire built, the tent up and all the preparations made for as comfortable a night as was possible in those frozen regions. It seemed a new life after the experiences of the past to get so much of comfort and such thoughtful and congenial companionship. The gentlemen with whom I had come in were kind and thoughtful, but I was the only lady in the party and female companionship becomes more desirable the farther one gets from civilization.

At Tagish, while we were waiting to get our boats numbered and thousands were in line in the barracks grounds, I noticed some peculiar goings-on just outside of the barracks and about 200 yards below. When the barracks gates were opened a certain number were let in and then the gates were closed and another thousand awaited their turn to get into the grounds.

An officer was walking to and fro some 200 yards below the barracks and occasionally a man would pass him and hand him a package without saying a word, and that same man could be seen in a short time going down the river. The package looked suspiciously like a bottle of whiskey.

This was evidently the way to facilitate the procuring of the necessary number without waiting an interminable time.

But while I had money I had none of the potent whiskey which seemed to be the "open sesame" to quick transit down the river.

Although it was a penal offense "for some" to take whiskey into the country, I had been told that "Black Sullivan" was taking a scow-load of whiskey into the Yukon on a special permit. So to him I hied me and unfolded my "tale of woe."

He was a fine specimen of the brunet type of Milesian, six feet tall, weighing 220 pounds, with white skin, luminous, dark, expressive eyes and hair wavy and black as a raven, and a heart in him as big as an ox.

He had been into the Yukon country before and was well known to all the miners. When I made my request he looked at me, with an air of grieved surprise and said, "As sure as my name is 'Black Sullivan' I haven't got a drop of whiskey."

I explained to him that I wanted to get a sick man through the line and it seemed that a bottle of whiskey was the only thing that would do it.

He looked me over and looked clear through me and then turning he pointed to his scow and said in a mellow tone of voice, "If you will go down there in a half-hour and feel in my coat pocket, you may find something."

I offered him the customary price, $5. He declined the money, saying, "No, just wish Black Sullivan a safe journey through the White Horse Rapids."

When I returned to the barracks I found the officer had been changed. Another was then on duty. I took the chances that the tariff was the same and as I went by him I handed him the bottle without a word.

He took it and the spell was broken. Loitering about, it was not long before a man approached me, took the names of our party and handed me the sign with the number of our boat upon it and evaporated.

This enabled us to get away at once and join the procession of boats down the river.

We first passed through Miles Canyon. The canyon is narrow, not over forty feet wide, and the current is very rapid. The walls of the canyon are about 600 feet high and the crevasse is a fissure of the rocks. After passing through this and shooting the Squaw Rapids, which are just below, we found a large red flag on which was inscribed "Danger about three miles below," and we knew that we must be near White Horse Rapids, which from the time of the starting on the trail had been the bugbear of every member of the party.

We were called ashore to the camp of the police and about 30 men who were acting as pilots and who were camped with them. We were told by the police that it was entirely unsafe to attempt to run the rapids without a pilot and that the charges were $25 for each boat.

The tariff had been so heavy and the various species of graft so continuous that most of the voyagers were at the end of their tether and to extract any more was like getting blood out of a stone.

Every one went down to the rapids and looked over the situation. They decided that all the women should go ashore and walk around the rapids, which was about half a mile, the men to take their chances and shoot the rapids with their boat-loads of provisions and miners' supplies. Our boat with the men went through the rapids. Myself and Mrs. Wilson started ahead with my dog Napoleon walking by my side along the bank. Napoleon paid no attention to any one going through until my first traveling companions, the Cady party, came shooting down the river. As they struck the rapids the spray completely submerged the boat and its occupants and Napoleon having evidently recognized his old friends, and fearing for their safety, emitted a howl of dismay, and without a moment's hesitation, plunged into the seething canyon.

The rapids were boiling and foaming and whirling but Napoleon was undaunted and was swept into the whirlpool. He spun around about twenty times until a compassionate man in a small boat went to his rescue. Napoleon managed to get out of the current and came ashore to me wagging his tail, sure of the approbation of affection with which I greeted him.

Those who first passed the rapids, our party among them, reached the placid water below in safety.

In mid-channel I discovered two things. First that the right and left-hand sides of the channel were entirely different. There must be some reason for it, I was sure. I walked below the rapids and looked up the stream. Suddenly the sun shone on the water at such an angle that I could see through and beneath the clear water to where at least two feet beneath the surface was a sharp-pointed and ragged rock in the middle of the channel. Then I watched the boats as they came down. I saw at once that the current set so that any boat of any size taking the left-hand channel would inevitably be drawn by the strong current on this rock and be destroyed, and while an Indian was cavorting about in the left-hand channel in a light canoe without accident it seemed to me he was being used as one uses a wooden decoy duck in the feeding grounds of the East, to convey to the people coming down that he was in the safe channel, whereas, with a heavily loaded boat, to follow him was impossible, and those who tried it found, no matter how strong and skilful, their boat drawn by that current was doomed to drift onto that sunken rock and be lost, while all on board must perish. I stood on the bank at an altitude of forty feet and saw the crowd of boats coming. The first to take the left-hand channel were fellow passengers with me from San Francisco. There were eight men in the boat, full of hope and joy at their approach to the gold-fields. They were all singing when the boat struck the sunken rock, reared into the air and went to pieces in a few minutes. Only one of the men came into the whirlpool after swimming the rapids.

Had it been possible to get a pole or a rope or anything that I could have reached ten feet to him I could have saved him, but none was available. He shouted his last messages to his mother and wife at me, and I buried my face in my hands to shut out the awful sight of a fellow creature struggling as he did against the inevitable. He must have swum around the whirlpool a dozen or more times after swimming through the rapids before his superb athletic frame gave in to the strain put upon it and he went down to his death. I hurried to the police station and asked them to send ropes and a small boat to be stationed at the whirlpool for life-saving purposes, which they did, and many were saved thereafter through this precautionary measure.

I then drew a map showing the channels and the position of this sunken rock, and returned to the camp above the rapids, where the men were waiting to come through. I sought out Black Sullivan first. He had asked me to wish him a safe passage of the rapids. I showed him my map and explained to him what I had seen and knew. We discussed the matter fully. Then he called Mr. Lippy, of Seattle, into the conference. Each had a big scow with a valuable cargo. Lippy's consisted of provisions, while Sullivan had a scow-load of whiskey worth a dollar a drink. Each had a crew of several men; and finally Sullivan took my advice, while Lippy laughed at the theories and insisted on taking the left channel, which he did. I started ahead to see them go through the rapids.

Lippy struck the place where the current separated, then took the left channel. Sullivan was immediately behind him and took the right-hand channel, passed safely through and emerged into the placid water below. Lippy had sixteen men rowing, and they were drilled to fill the boat with great power, which he figured would overcome any current he could encounter.

But he had made a mistake, and when he came to that current setting upon the rock his crew of oarsmen were as helpless as children, and the scow was driven onto the rock and split in two, both halves standing up in the air until they were almost perpendicular.

The crew fortunately got entangled in the ropes with which the cargo was fastened, and most of them were rescued from the whirlpool, into which they had drifted. I was called to care for one of his men who had broken his wrist, and to whom I attended as well as I could under the circumstances. Both Lippy and Black Sullivan had a personal following, and this led to their selecting the routes of their respective chieftains through the rapids. Those who followed Sullivan went through as safely as he did, and a few of Lippy's henchmen got through, though the majority were wrecked. An amusing incident was the case of a man in a small boat who struck the rock and was hurled high in the air. When he came down he landed safely in a big boat in the right-hand channel, while his boat and provisions were lost. It must be remembered that the procession of boats was continuous; once started there was no stopping. You got in line and there was no place to land until the rapids were passed and you were beyond the whirlpool. As soon as we could, Mrs. Wilson and myself started up the canyon. We had both refused to go on, feeling that it was our duty to do all we could to warn the crowd that was yet to come of the unknown evils which confronted them. Those who got through safely went on as fast as possible to the gold-fields, caring nothing for those who were left behind.

In their imagination they saw gold nuggets piled up like paving-stones awaiting their arrival and selection. The ocean voyage, the Chilcoot Pass, the White Horse Rapids, all lost their horrors. They were almost in sight of the gold-fields and the Midas-like wealth of which they had heard and which was the magnet that had drawn them from civilization to the borders of the Arctic Circle.

The story of the making of the first American flag for the army of the thirteen colonies at the time of the Revolutionary War is too well known to need anything but a reference, and this is the story of the first United States flag made in the Klondike.

After we had succeeded in stopping the mad rush and persuading those we could get at to take the proper channel we sewed sugar- and floursacks together and printed upon it, "Danger—Keep to the right," and hung it on a pole projecting from the bank over the water just above where the channel divided, in plain view of every boat that came down the stream. While we were doing this the pilots were in consultation, evidently displeased at our action. Shortly thereafter I saw one of the pilots sneakingly pull the flag in so close to the bank that approaching boats could not see it till they were directly under it. Then again the Indian appeared in his canoe in the left channel. I was then satisfied in my own mind that the Indian was being used as a decoy to lure men to death who would not or could not pay the required fee to the pilots. I hired a Norwegian, a young man in whom I had confidence, to guard the signal-flag all night, which he did till the crowd had passed in safety, and we joined the procession the next morning and floated down the river to the golden country still farther north. We now confronted a voyage of six hundred miles upon the Yukon River before reaching Dawson and the gold-fields. The days went gliding by, and we enjoyed every hour of that wonderful journey. The mountains were covered with wild game—the moose, mountain-sheep, cinnamon and black bear, black and silver gray fox, the latter, one of the most beautiful of fur-bearing animals.

The many rivers emptying into the Yukon are large and beautiful mountain-streams.

The current was never less than six miles an hour, and when the channel narrowed the current carried us along at twenty miles an hour. The mountain scenery was sublime. The descent from our point of embarkation to the coast was abrupt, as is all the Pacific coast of the Northwest, and this will account for our rapid progress without effort.

We traveled for about three hundred miles, day and night, and then by agreement we all stopped for a night's rest. We made camp on the right-hand bank of the Yukon River, and near heavily timbered land, where a small band of Indians had also stopped for the night. There we built a big camp-fire and had the first hot food and drink we had enjoyed for many long days.

My friend Mrs. Wilson and myself agreed to sit up and watch the midnight sun. Every man in camp was soon wrapped in profound slumber, and we two women were wrapped in that silence which is found alone in the mountains.

The ocean is always restless and usually noisy, but the calm of the mountains in that uninhabited cold country is indescribably impressive.

Suddenly I heard a peculiar noise. Something had fallen into the water. I thought some man had been wrecked in his boat just up the river. But I could do nothing except go quickly to the tent of Fred Baker, Mrs. Wilson's brother, and awaken him quietly. He raised the flap of his tent and looked up the river. He saw what proved to be a large moose swimming for the opposite shore. Seizing his rifle he opened fire. The men each had their guns by their side, although they had taken off their clothes for the first time in weeks, and thinking they were the subjects of an Indian attack they began shooting in every direction without waiting to find out what they were shooting at. Fred hit the moose at his first shot, and it came drifting down, oblivious of the bullets that rained around it, until opposite to where we were encamped, and we drew the carcass to shore and proceeded to skin it and cut it up. Fair play is a jewel. We ladies were entitled, "so the crowd said," to the hide, horns and this great carcass. We donated it to the camp. So we had "all of us" a feast. The men, who had little on but their undershirts, kept shooting at the carcass for nearly ten minutes, when we drew it ashore and skinned it. There were only three bullet-holes in the hide. Most of the white men and all of the Indians each thought the other had inaugurated hostilities, and both took to the tall timber, fearing results.

In less than an hour we began preparations for a "Pot Latch" or great feast. The sun was up and shining bright. The men who had taken to the woods, hundreds of them, were gathered in as they shouted and yelled from the woods for something to cover their nakedness. They were with the Indians, and all of them were in a denuded state. We sent our Indian guide to tell them that we were not there to steal their game, but on our way to the gold-fields, and would be off before sunset. We told the guide to invite the tribe to join us in the feast of moose-meat, so they sent scouts out in every direction to gather them in.

At noon we huddled together around a huge camp-fire over which was suspended the carcass of the moose, and cutting off chunks and strips we fell to eating it and enjoyed our gastronomic orgy with the zest derived from months of self-denial. We had not tasted fresh meat in four months and had our last decent meal in Victoria.

If you have never seen an Indian eat you will find it hard to believe the capacity of an Indian's stomach. I passed it to them, and saw them in many cases eat not less than ten pounds of roast meat. It was a question in my mind how the stomach could accommodate itself to such a quantity of food at one time. At the close of the feast we divided the meat remaining among the Indians and our own party, and again embarked in our boats and floated on down the river.

We were still 300 miles from the gold-fields. The next stop we made was at Selkirk, an Indian trading-post. There we found one white man, a Mr. Pitt, a man of wonderful character and integrity, which endeared him to whites and Indians alike. He had been there many years and had the most complete influence over the Indians, and was the only person in the country who could control them. He explained to us the mysteries of the Totem poles which stand at the wigwams of the chiefs. The carving is in the nature of a genealogical tree, and tells the family history to the Indians passing by of those who dwell therein.

As we drifted down the rapid stream and swung around an abrupt turn in the river we could see the mountain called Big Scookum many miles in the distance. It overhangs Dawson City.

Mr. Pitt told us, years and years ago, when the Selkirk Indians were holding a council of war at the foot of this mountain planning an attack on the Mallamoot tribe, while in conference there was an avalanche of rock, which we could see, and it buried beneath it all the warriors of the tribe. It required the growth of a new generation before their plans could be carried out.

One day more, drifting with the current, and we reached Dawson, which is in Canadian territory. Here most of the crowd finished their journey. A few went on down the Yukon River about a hundred miles to Eagle City, Alaska, preferring to prospect for gold where the stars and stripes float over Uncle Sam's domain.

# CHAPTER VI

WHEN we landed in Dawson there had been, a few days previous, the usual flood that follows the going of the ice out of the rivers. There was a foot of mud and silt over the entire city. This consisted of about 500 tents and a few log houses, only two of which were of important size. The Alaska Commercial Company's store was a one-story building about 40 x 60 feet, and the Yukon Hotel, which was about 75 feet long by 16 wide and two stories in height.

Here I separated from my fellow-travelers, who went into camp, and I took up my quarters in the hotel with about 60 miners. The proprietor was a German named Louis Schonburg, a genial host who looked after my comfort in every way possible in that country. The house was furnished with bunks—not bedsteads—and each room had one rough stool, and for illumination a tallow candle in a miner's candlestick stuck in the logs.

The rooms were partitioned off with calico about eight feet high, and as for washing facilities, they had none. I went down stairs and washed with the miners and wiped on the general towel. All supplies were exhausted at the store. I could not get a yard of muslin or anything for towels, so I had to make the best of the existing circumstances. We found about one-half of the population sick with the scurvy.

The house was made of logs and chinked with wood moss. The roof was made of poles upon which were laid layers of the moss, and then dirt was thrown on this moss.

In the dining-room we had steel knives and forks, and rough tables without cloths or napkins. We ate from tin plates. Our menu was bacon and beans, bread and coffee, without either milk or sugar, three times a day. For this luxurious fare we paid $2.50 per meal and $4 per night for our bunk.

I made arrangements that first night to go up Bonanza Creek to see a mine. I walked around the greater part of the night, the sun being obscured only a little over an hour during the whole time.

Along about eleven o'clock at night I was pacing up and down a board walk between the hotel and a row of tents pitched on the opposite side. I saw several miners sitting out near a large tent talking about the early days in Montana. They spoke of Custer's last fight at the massacre of the Little Big Horn.

I found a label from a tomato can, and as it was the only available literature in the country I pretended to be studying it as an excuse for my listening to the conversation.

The member of the group who attracted my attention most was well dressed, sporting immaculate linen and an air of civilization which I had missed for months. He was "dressed up," as the miners say, in tailor-made clothes, and I fastened my eyes upon him. An Indian named "Skookum Jim," just in from the trail, spoke to him, and I was astonished to hear him speaking the Indian dialect as fluently as he did English. He was not only noticeable for his dress, but for his personality and his superb physique. Above medium height, with high forehead and deepset, steel-blue eyes, his chin was square and indicative of the determination of the man. His hair was of a light golden hue, only slightly wavy and very fine and well-kept.

My curiosity was aroused as to what this man could be doing amid the rough surroundings of a mining-camp. A man who I afterward learned was Jeff Talbort raised his voice and said, "You remember the night you and I and Louie Kabell rode into Sitting Bull's camp, and how, when we found the trap which we had stumbled into, we covered the old Indian war-horse with our guns and backed out with Sitting Bull, the old hypocrite, praying for us, saying that was all he could do; but we got out safely all the same.

"I never heard you talk Indian as you did that night, when you told old Sitting Bull he must give orders to his men to escort us safely out of camp and turn us loose."

"Yes," said the man in the "Sunday-clothes," "that was the time when Johnny Manning was sheriff of the Black Hills country. And, by the way, I hear Johnny has hit the trail and is on his way in.

"At that time a white woman had been scalped

in the Cooly not far from our camp. When a white woman was scalped Manning got up a posse and went out after the miscreant. Johnny was sure white, and the bravest man I ever knew."

One of the men in the crowd said, "How about Jack Crawford, the poet scout?"

"Well," replied the man in the boiled shirt, "the bravest thing Jack Crawford ever did was to write a poem on Johnny Manning. It begins something like this:

"Good-bye, you brave old pioneer,
    There never breathed a truer friend
Than honest Johnny, none more dear
    Where honesty and justice blend.
We knew you on the wild frontier,
    When savage foe and outlaws, too,
Were curbed and cowed in abject fear,
    Because to duty you were true.

"We knew you when your cabin door
    Was open wide to those in need;
And bounteously from out your store
    You gave, that hungry men might feed.
Ah, Johnny Manning, friend of mine,
    You'll die as poor as Job's old fowl;
But on the heavenly range you'll shine,
    While devil broncho-busters howl."

I sat until nearly midnight listening to a conversation which covered astronomy, navigation and scientific gold-mining.

Mr. Staley, with whom I had arranged to go up Bonanza, called me, saying it was time for us to start into the gold-district. We traveled over the only trail there was in the country. It was a corduroy road laid upon the tops of a vegetable formation called "niggerheads," which were all over that country. These niggerheads grow up in marsh lands, and are from one to two feet in height. They grow about two feet apart and are covered with moss. At the base they are of good size and come to a point at the surface, being surrounded by water and a most disagreeable moss formation woven in and out among them.

This road was built on the niggerheads for a distance of a half-mile to the foot of the mountain that overhangs the city of Dawson. There a road, cut through the gravel and ice, wound around the mountain for another mile, and you arrived on the abrupt banks of the Klondike River, which empties into the Yukon River at Dawson.

Here we crossed the Klondike on a ferry, in which the primitive rope was used to keep the boat in the channel, and struck a corduroy road which led up Bonanza Creek to the mines. This road was under construction, and after five miles we were compelled to step from niggerhead to niggerhead, where a misstep would plunge us into water up to our knees.

The distance from Dawson to the camp at Grand Forks, a point where Eldorado empties into Bonanza and where Upper Bonanza empties into Lower Bonanza, was 14 miles.

At Grand Forks was a camp of about 200 tents, and a Mrs. Bell Mulrooney had a tent hotel of her own, which would accommodate about a dozen people, and where I became a guest. In a radius of two miles from the Forks where the camp was located the richest auriferous deposits were found. The places were known as Eldorado, French Hill, Gold Hill, Big Scookum, Little Scookum, Upper and Lower Bonanza, and Dick Low's Fraction, which was the richest piece of ground in the whole country. I have seen $600 washed out of one medium-sized pan of dirt.

About half a mile below this point, on Lower Bonanza, the first discovery of gold was made in the spring of 1897. This trip was the worst of my many experiences. We were from one o'clock in the early morning to ten o'clock at night making this journey on foot, and I was legweary and footsore when I struck the mines.

After a night's rest I started to look for a gold-mine. I had traveled so far and endured so much that I was quite ready to turn my face to the rising sun and return to my home and friends. But I wanted to see a gold-mine at least before doing so. Seeing some men working over what I afterward learned was a sluice-box I strolled over to their claim. They were cordial and in a rude way gallant. They invited me to wash out a pan of dirt, but as I was ignorant of the technique I made bad work of it. The pan got away from me and turned bottomside up in the tub of water in which I was panning. This greatly amused the workmen. Then one of them showed me how to manipulate the pan and found a shovelful of dirt. I washed out four and one-half ounces of gold, worth $68, and in accordance with the miners' customs, I was presented with the proceeds of my first pan-out.

I felt delicate about accepting this gold, but they insisted, saying there was plenty more where that came from, and at the same time a man stepped into his tent and brought out a frying-pan filled with nuggets ranging in size from a small marble to a walnut. Then he took up a riffle and showed me gold as coarse as wheat and corn-grains an inch deep in the bottom of the box.

Mr. Staley called to me to go with him a short distance to the Berry claim on Eldorado Creek, where we saw a big clean-up going on, and before nightfall they had cleaned up over $60,000. They did not have bags enough to put it in, and bread-pans, frying-pans and even rubber boots were pressed into service and made receptacles for this great wealth.

I stood speechless as I saw this treasure taken from the ground at an average of from one to four feet from the surface. The ground was to be had for the staking under the law, and I had a miner's license to stake, which I had purchased at Victoria, paying a fee of ten dollars to the government. A claim was then 500 feet up and down the creek and extending from rim rock to rim rock, which was about 600 feet across the creek.

Even the sight of the gold did not allure me. So great had been the hardships which I had undergone that to return home was the one desirable thing in life.

Had I known how much more terrible were the experiences which awaited me than those I had passed through no earthly power could have kept me in Dawson, Yukon Territory of Canada. I wanted to stake a claim under my license before leaving the country with a view not to working but to selling it. But the claims that were on the "pay streak" in the creek they told me were all taken. On the hillside the only claim which had panned out worth staking was the Travarra claim on Gold Hill.

I did not want to throw away my right of location on barren ground and I asked a practical old miner this question: "How can you tell where the pay streak runs?"

He replied, "Oh, that is easy."

"Then there are no claims around the Travarra claim worth staking?" I suggested.

"Oh, no," he replied; "you see, the gravel which carries the gold all slipped into the creek except at that point where the Travarra claim is located."

So I did not stake near that claim as I wished to do. But some three months after I bought a portion of the claim adjoining the Travarra claim, for which I paid $4,000. I could have staked the whole claim for nothing had not these old miners who really knew nothing about the pay streak steered me off.

In less than three months every **foot of that** hillside was yielding big returns.

On the creek between two rich claims a blank was found (that is an unproductive piece of ground).

All over the Klondike this was the case, that one claim would yield richly and the adjoining claim be barren. No one can tell whether there is gold on a claim or not without first prospecting it, and no one should ever buy one without taking that precaution. Gold is where you find it, the Bible says. Regardless of the demonstrated richness of the country, my resolution to return home was not shaken by the wealth I saw being taken out of the ground. Through the courtesy of Mr. Staley I was furnished with a packhorse to return to Dawson. But the animal would break through the trail, and it proved to be much more tiresome than to walk. As I rode into the city of tents and drew rein in front of my hotel, I was assisted by Mr. Louis Schonburg to dismount, and I noticed my man with the store clothes unloading gold in bags, taking it into his tent opposite. His clean-up was so great that it took seven mules to carry it into camp. I asked who he was, and Mr. Schonburg replied, "That is Edward MacConnell, the laziest man that ever rode into a mining-camp. But he knows a mine when he sees it, and that dust you have and the first you ever panned out came out of one of his mines. He built the only trail worthy the name in this region, and he built a bridge across the Klondike River which cost him

$37,000 and which went out with the ice a few days ago. He now owns and operates the ferry across the Klondike.

"I knew him in Montana when he was collector of customs in that State. He was nicknamed by his friends 'Easy Money,' on account of his liberality. He bought the first and only steamboat built in the country, which was constructed during the winter at Lake Bennett by Captain John Irving and named Willie Irving for the latter's little son.

"Mr. MacConnell says he is going to open navigation and run boats up the Yukon River to the White Horse Rapids. But no one believes that the navigation of the river against the tide and current is a possible thing."

I said, "Do not boats go up the river now?"

"No," said he, "now people come down in small boats, as you did, and the scows are broken up, as they are of no use once you are in the country."

This was a surprise to me. It never had occurred to me that I was a prisoner in the Klondike. Only when the river was frozen over was it possible to get out by going up the river, and that would be by traveling on the ice. The boats could and did come up the river from St. Michael's in September and early October, but the rest of the time they were ice-bound in the north. In the spring, when the ice goes out, there are usually heavy rains. For three days it rained, and while I was in bed asleep the rain broke through my moss roof and drenched me. I had no change of dry clothing, everything was wet. We could not dry our garments, and men and women went about like drenched rats. For three days and nights it continued to pour in torrents. and all over the floors of tents the water stood two feet deep.

# CHAPTER VII

WHEN I reached Dawson on my return from Bonanza, a period of only two days had elapsed, but in that time those who had followed us arrived at Dawson, and the inhabitants had increased in that brief interval from about 500 to over 12,000 souls. Tents covered the plains between the river and the foot of the mountain, and all was bustle and confusion. Just as soon as the water receded, a period of not more than a few hours, h—— broke loose in that camp. Drinking-saloons of the Red Dog variety were opened in profusion, and in them drinking and gambling were rife every hour in the twenty-four. The sun shining all night as well as all day kept the ball rolling, and people would go three days and nights without sleeping.

The miners came down from the creeks every time they had a clean-up, and brought their gold with them, spending most of it in dissipation. I asked Schonburg where they deposited their gold. He started to tell me something, but a man approached and he shut up like a clam. Finally we were alone and he beckoned me into his room. He was embarrassed at having a lady in his room (at least he pretended to be), and quickly lifted the curtain nailed around his bunk and motioned me to look. There, in tin cans and sacks, was a fortune. "Over $300,000 under there," he whispered.

There were no banks and no safes in Dawson at that time, but a man's money anywhere he stowed it was safer than in a bank, as future events proved. The camp was ruled by a vigilance committee and governed by miners' unwritten laws. Any man who stole his neighbor's gold would have been hung higher than Haman on detection. It remained for civilization to bring with it thieves and robbers.

I remained at the primitive hotel for the next ten days. I spent most of my time wandering about looking over the ground and sizing up the situation.

Among the recent arrivals were that class of immoral women who always rush into a new mining-camp, and in a few days dance-halls were opened on the main thoroughfares for the entertainment of the miners who came to Dawson from the mines. The women in these dance-halls were not what you would call raving beauties, but there was a frank exposure of such charms as they imagined they had, for they wore dresses abbreviated at both ends, thus displaying their necks and arms and their legs up to their knees. They were largely Canucks, or Canadian French, and they ranged in ages from children 12 years old to old women of 60, gray-haired but hopeful.

The music was furnished by a cracked fiddle, and the price charged for the privilege of dancing with these sirens was five dollars a head. At one end of the room was a bar where whiskey was retailed at one dollar a drink, and it was customary to buy a drink for the girl you danced with, if you did not, as almost all the men did, treat the whole crowd. One night there was an invasion by a big, rawboned Scotchman with a fine load of what he called "whuskey" in his skin. He volunteered to dance the Highland Fling, and did so, encouraged by the jeers, laughter and applause of the crowd. When he had finished he shouted out, "Now I want some one to donce with, and if you have any one here who can donce, trot her out—any old pig is good enough for me."

There was so much money in the camp that everybody was good-natured, and the rough-house and gun-plays common to mining-camps were conspicuously absent from our lives in Dawson. The life was out of doors and easily seen from the streets. The floors alone were of wood, and they were roofed and walled in with canvas—gambling-dens, boozing-stalls and dance-halls alike.

In about two weeks an illness broke out in the camp, and I was called to prescribe for the wife of a Canuck known as French Curly. I found her in a high fever. It was neither typhoid nor typhus fever. It was a new phase of illness to me, as the bowels were involved seriously. I am of the opinion that the decayed vegetation and the moss and the hot sun pouring down at noonday upon them brought about a deadly miasmatic condition which threatened to decimate the town. The victims were attacked as suddenly as cholera patients are. In a few days about half the population, consisting of 12,000 souls, was stricken, and about one-third of the population died. Many of them left no means of identification and are mourned by their relatives in the East as among the unknown dead. This epidemic lasted from the last of June until the middle of August, when, the weather growing cold, the moss was frozen at night, and the sickness ended as suddenly as it had begun.

I rented a tent, ten by twelve feet, and paid $65 per month for the same. It was of canvas, with a board floor raised two feet from the ground. It was directly adjoining the hotel. Here I opened an office for the practice of my profession. There were two physicians besides myself who had come into the country, but both of them got the gold fever and went up Bonanza Creek prospecting. From one of them I purchased his store of drugs and surgical instruments, and hung out my shingle.

When the epidemic broke out I turned my office into a hospital and filled it with patients. I put my clothing and everything else I could find under their heads for pillows. I had a box in the center of the floor to sit on that was my only furniture.

John Rosine, of Seattle, and now a millionaire steamship-owner and president of the Northwestern Steamship Company, was one of my patients, and lay on that same floor in this rude hospital and was "broke to cases."

For three weeks I never slept day or night, watching over and caring for these unfortunate men. I finally got so worn and weary that I could not eat. I offered a young man a hundred dollars to sit up with the sick just one night so I could get one night's rest and sleep. He declined, saying he would not stay an hour in that tent for a thousand dollars, much less all night. He feared that the fever was contagious, and hastened away.

I walked along the board walk and saw the people dead and dying in nearly every tent, and for the first and only time in my life I became absolutely panic-stricken. I felt that I must get away from that place, and that soon, or I should die myself. But how? I finally decided to get into a small boat, of which there were plenty scattered along the shore, and float down the river. I could not bring myself to leave my dog Napoleon behind, and so took the risk of his upsetting the boat, knowing from experience that if he did so he would land me safe on shore. I packed my dressing-bag and dressed for the journey. Just as I started to leave the tent I turned for a last farewell look around.

It was midnight. At that moment a Mr. Joel, a relative of the late Barney Barnato, opened his eyes and spoke for the first time in three weeks, saying, "Water, water." I had found him unconscious under a fly-tent and got Mr. Franks, the jeweler, to help bring him into my tent. I put down my bag to give him a drink, intending to go on as soon as he had slaked his thirst. But the expression of his large brown eyes and the smile of gratitude that came over his face when I gave him water encouraged me, and I resolved to stay by them. I then noticed that a man named James Smith, of Oregon, who was a friend of Mr. and Mrs. Wilson, was beckoning me to come to him. He was so weak I had to go down on my knees to catch his words. He wanted the pictures of his wife and baby, and I handed them to him. He gazed intently at the portraits, kissed them, reached out and took my hand in his, and in a few minutes he had passed over the "great divide."

Father Judge, of the Roman Catholic Church, came into camp from the Mission of the Holy Cross, in Alaska, about 1,700 miles down the river from Dawson. He came up the river traveling over the ice. He opened a hospital, which he located at the foot of the avalanche where the Indians were lost. Here he pitched several tents, one 40 by 60 feet, and ministered to the sick, shrived the dying and buried the dead. This good man did not spare himself at any time, and when the epidemic subsided he built a church on the spot where the tent hospital had stood. He was universally beloved, and when death overtook him he was buried in the church he had built, mourned alike by Protestants and Catholics.

The gold was plentiful, and yet many a man died before he got an ounce or a mine. And yet where they were buried the auriferous soil was so rich in gold that their graves are decorated with nuggets. There was no time or opportunity during the epidemic for questions of creed. Catholics and heretics alike lie side by side awaiting the call. At least this must be said for most of these brave men that they laid down their lives not for selfish reasons, but in hope of some day, soon, taking back to their homes the gold which would ensure the future independence of their loved ones.

## CHAPTER VIII

IT WAS nearing the last of August, and the ice had gone out of the rivers and lakes, and a grand rush into the country began. Not only miners of adventurous nature, such as had come in from the trail when I did, but professional men, doctors and lawyers, came. The gold-commissioner at Dawson opened an office. Judge Dugas opened his court. Law and order and stealing began as is customary under civilization.

The first flagrant acts were committed by Judge Amie Calixie Dugas. He put men to work on a claim on Dominion Creek, and when they had taken out the best of the pay-dirt and had cleaned up, he took the gold and transferred the mine to his son, Amie Calixie the younger. The miners tried for four years in the courts and by petitioning the government at Ottawa to recover their wages, but without success. This inaugurated the period of corruption which ensued.

The ground in the Yukon never thaws out more than a couple of feet, even in the summer months. The method employed in mining is different from placer-mining or quartz-mining in other parts of the world. The ground has to be thawed out before you can get the gold from it. Huge fires are built on rocks, and then the ground is steamed. Fortunately timber is most plentiful, and to be had at first for the cutting, so that there was little labor and no expense in procuring all the timber necessary for this method of mining. The dirt in summer was often under water, as the melting glaciers poured their water into the shaft. Sometimes the water could be pumped out; at others they would have to shut down the work until the ground froze solid again.

It was about this time that I first met Mr. MacConnell. I was invited into his tent to see a large clean-up, and he was presented to me by one Lafayette Hamilton.

We saw the clean-up, and there was a large dishpan full of gold-dust and nuggets heaped up, pressed down and running over. I was asked to select nuggets enough to make me a bracelet, which I did, and which I still have. I was also invited to go in company with two other ladies on the trial trip of the new steamer Willie Irving. It took place at midnight. It was a moonlight night, and Mr. MacConnell invited the ladies into the pilot-house with him. He was owner, captain and pilot of the boat. No boat had ever been above that point, and the first five miles was the worst water between Dawson and White Horse Rapids. Slowly the steamer gathered headway and, gradually increasing her speed, glided up the river. The problem of the navigation of the upper Yukon had been solved. In a few days he took her up to White Horse Rapids. Her passengers then transferred to other boats on the lakes, and in this way they got out in three weeks instead of five months, going down the river by St. Michael's.

This achievement was naturally most displeasing to the big companies who were then operating big steamships on the lower river to St. Michael's, thence to Seattle and San Francisco. These were compelled (at least most of them) to haul up and dry-rot.

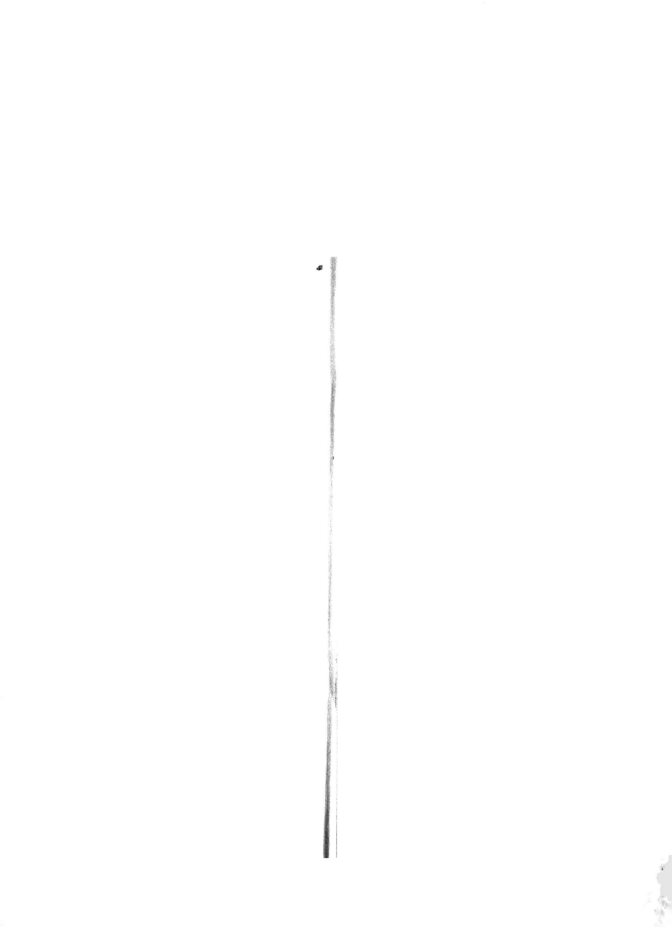

# CHAPTER IX

THE organization of the Yukon government was made at Ottawa under the Liberal rule about this time by the appointment of a council consisting of Judge Dugas, Governor Ogilvie, who was acting as surveyor on the boundary line when the gold-fields were discovered; Major Wood, in command of the Northwest Mounted Police, and Mr. Senkler, the gold commissioner. Two others were appointed, but they were honorable men and had but little use for the rest of the gang.

These appointments were made by Clifford Sifton, who was at that time Minister of the Interior at Ottawa. From this it will be seen that the people in the Yukon had nothing whatever to say as to their government or their rulers. They collected a royalty of ten per cent of all the gold taken out in the territory. Later on this was reduced to five per cent, but not till the mines were nearly worked out and the gold output largely reduced.

The Canadian Bank of Commerce late in the summer of the year opened a branch bank in Dawson. Up to this time there had been absolutely no banking facilities in the Territory. The bank in Ottawa sent in H. T. Wills as its resident manager, and O. H. Clark was the lawyer for the bank and the power behind the throne.

He was a relative of Clifford Sifton (so the papers said), who was then Minister of the Interior. O. H. Clark ruled things with a rod of iron. He controlled the officers of the Territory, with the single exception of the sheriff, "Dad" Eilbeck, who was appointed to his office for life, and being a man who was "sure white" in every way and one of the best men that was ever sent into the Yukon Territory, he declined to be dictated to by O. H. Clark, who boasted of being the "political boss" of the Territory.

The truth of this statement will be made apparent by the recital of the facts which follow.

The personality of O. H. Clark was indicative of his over-bearing disposition. Rascality was written on his face. As I have said, he ruled things with a rod of iron, and to such an extent did he carry his high-handed proceedings that he walked into the courts and dictated openly to the judges on the bench, and so terrorized were they by him that they did his bidding absolutely without protest.

Sent in by Clifford Sifton to do his bidding, he served his master well.

The gold commissioner's office was as much under his thumb as the courts and judges. In order to facilitate the rascality in the gold commissioner's office no records were kept, as is customary in such offices. After a man had staked a claim he would give another man his power of attorney, enabling him to do the representation work, and go to another camp, or perhaps out of the country to visit his family. Every year a new certificate must be issued and an affidavit filed that $200 worth of work had been done on the claim; otherwise, in case of failure to comply with this law, the title to the mine would revert to the government. The power of attorney, in the case of a good claim, was taken from the pigeonhole, and before the man could get another from the owner the title to the mine was lost and the conspirators would jump the claim. This was one of the schemes. If these legal documents were pigeonholed in a vault they could be removed at the will of O. H. Clark. In one case I have the positive proof that when Clark wanted a big judgment which he got against Edward MacConnell, a miner, the wink was tipped to the court, and when the judge issued a subpoena *duces tecum,* commanding the production of the document in court, it could not be found, and its existence was denied. It was a lease in evidence that had been taken from the vault by O. H. Clark and held out till after the judgment was given to him; then he returned it to the vault again. Many cases like this occurred. The American miner sacrificed all his property and left Canada on this account, saying he would not invest money where fraudulent acts like these prevailed.

These frauds and others too numerous to mention aroused the deep resentment of the miners, and they called an indignation meeting in front of the Northern Commercial Company's store. The miners were called in from the creeks, and nearly 10,000 persons were in front of the stores. A young politician and miner named

Joseph Andrew Clarke made a ringing speech condemning the government officials, and he did not hesitate to call them liars and thieves. Public feeling ran high, and there were not a few who counseled violent measures in reprisal for the wrongs inflicted on them. At eleven o'clock at night they formed in line and started to attack the barracks of the Northwest Mounted Police, of whom there were fewer than 100 at that particular time.

A big Scotchman, a man past middle age, named Colonel MacGregor, nicknamed the "Mysterious Man," called a halt and then made the miners abandon their designs on the barracks. MacGregor was a leader born and a most popular man—a man of good judgment usually, but who admitted to me three years after this occurrence that he had erred in judgment at this time. He was a mystery, since he had no mine, no store, nor any known occupation. Later Judge Dugas called him a conservative spy on the public street, and MacGregor chased him into his own court, where he took refuge in his private room behind barred doors. The latter swore vengeance in terms "not loud but deep."

These few facts will give an idea of the conditions prevailing in Dawson at this time.

The miners had sent a protest signed by about 2,000 to Ottawa to the head of the government asking that Judge Dugas be removed from the bench. The result of this was that while prior to this the miners had only to deal with the mounted police, a detachment of regular troops was sent into the camp, with cannon and a battery of artillery, commanded by Colonel Steele. An arsenal was established and garrisoned. This body of men were fine fellows.

Everything quieted down and large permanent structures went up taking the place of the tents. The logs were sawed into lumber by sawmills that had been brought in over the ice. The price was excessive, $600 a thousand, and $1.25 a pound was charged for carrying it up to the mines on Bonanza, a distance of about 14 miles.

After the petition had reached Ottawa an ordinance was passed forbidding any government official, owning mining property. Just previous to this time a man was tried for an attempt to murder a miner on his claim. He was recommended to the mercy of the court and the judge acquitted him. In the meantime a transfer was made by this man of a half-interest in a rich claim to a woman. It came to light later on that this woman in whom the title was vested was the judge's wife. He had taken title from the prisoner before his trial in his wife's maiden name.

Nearly every government official was represented by a mining agent. Fred Burnham represented Lord Roberts and left the claim that he had charge of on Gold Hill to go to the Boer War as a scout for the English government. Captain Norwood, the papers said, represented Premier Laurier and had charge of several of the richest claims in the Territory.

Fred C. Wade, who was Queen's Counsel, and Judge Craig came into the Territory at this time, sent in response to a petition filed at Ottawa by the miners asking for the removal of Judge Dugas. Dugas was not removed, but he took leave and visited Ottawa, being gone several months. During his absence Judge Craig held court in his stead.

The camp had now become so healthy, owing to sanitary measures, that there was almost absolutely no demand for the services of a physician.

"Othello's occupation gone," I was offered a position by Mr. MacConnell. He had just completed building the Melbourne Hotel, a log building three stories high, containing 27 rooms; a huge caravansary for that country and which had cost him $36,000.

An idea of the cost of things in that country is afforded by the fact that each pane of glass 10 x 12 inches cost $5; a broom cost an ounce, which was $16; a can of oysters $25; a bottle of champagne $35; half a spring chicken, one ounce.

I weighed all the gold-dust that came into the hotel and kept it under my bed. It was left with me for safe-keeping by the miners. I have had over $2,000,000 in my care at one time. I handled all the money of Mr. MacConnell arising from his mines, steamboats, ferries and the hotel. I kept the books, acted as private secretary for several of the miners as well as for Mr. MacConnell, and received from him $500 per month. I have received from the miners over $2,000 a month in nuggets for weighing and taking care of their gold till they could take it out of the country on the steamboats.

At the same time my mines were yielding big returns and in a short time I bought the Melbourne Hotel from Mr. MacConnell, paying $32,000 for the property.

Then my real trouble began. Mr. H. T. Wills, manager of the Canadian Bank of Commerce branch in Dawson, came to me. He was a grand man in every sense of the word. He wanted to buy the property for a banking-house, it being by far the most desirable property and location in the city. He began by offering me $23,000 for the whole property for which I had paid $32,000 a short time before. I was satisfied from his small offer that he had been sent to me by O. H. Clark, the political boss. Mr. Wills advised me to take the offer and leave Dawson, saying it was no place for a woman of education and refinement. I refused to either get out of the camp or to sell my property, especially at any such sacrifice, while the camp was booming as it was at this time.

Mr. Wills was a man of the strictest integrity and practiced fair dealing with everyone. He was beloved by all the miners. He had done more than any one man in the camp to build up the city and develop the resources of the mines. Knowing this I was at a loss to know why he so earnestly advised me to leave the place, saying it was no place for a decent woman. He told me he was going to resign as manager of the bank for he could not stand it to see his friends who had always treated him fairly and squarely taken advantage of. Had I known the meaning of his words and their significance, which he dared not make plainer, I should have taken his advice and sacrificed my property and left the camp. But I had confidence in the government at that time and went on to face the most painful and dangerous experiences of my life, and my escape from being murdered by one of the gang was little short of miraculous.

A few days after this conversation with Mr. Wills the authorities began the erection of a two-story water-house in the public street, directly in front of my hotel and within ten feet of the entrance door. The purpose of this house was to store water in the upper half and keep it from freezing by fires on the ground floor. Here the people came to get their water supply when the thermometer was far below zero, and they used the sidewalks in front of my hotel entrance to rest their cans, barrels and buckets. Prior to this the people had gotten their water by cutting holes in the ice out of the Klondike River. An ordinance was passed forbidding the taking of water from any place except this water-tower and a tariff was fixed of 25 cents a bucket.

Some men who tried to defy this ordinance and take water from the Klondike at will were arrested and sent to jail by the "Organized Official Bandits."

They claimed as an excuse for this high-handed proceeding that the water of the Klondike, which had a current of 30 miles an hour at the point where the water was taken, as well as a gravel bottom and water as clear as crystal, was not fit for use and that they were protecting the health of the town as well as filling their own pockets.

They had carelessly put their well down about 200 feet from the Yukon River banks, exactly over the large cesspool used to dump the slops during the terrible epidemic, and from this hole they supplied the town with water, compelling, by "law and evidence," every one to pay 25 cents a bucket for the same, till within a short time the epidemic broke out again and the well was abandoned. They then pumped the water for their water-house from the Klondike.

I instructed my lawyer, F. C. Wade, who was also Queen's Counsel and prosecuting attorney, to bring a suit to cause the removal of the water-house from in front of my hotel, on the ground that it was a public nuisance, was trespassing on a public thoroughfare and was injuring my business as a hotel-keeper by obstructing egress and ingress and the view from the windows.

The case came up in Judge Craig's court and my lawyer elicited the fact that Governor Ogilvie owned a controlling interest in the water-works. All the officials denied having any interest in the water-works and water-house.

Mr. Wade demanded an order for the production of the books and papers. At first this was refused. Finally Judge Craig granted the order and they were forced to produce the books, which revealed the fact that the controlling interest belonged to Governor Ogilvie, and the balance of the stock to his personal friends in the ring.

In Judge Craig's decision he said the water-house was a public nuisance, and ordered it removed within a reasonable time—30 days—or the defendant to be held for contempt of court and committed.

The forcing into the court of the books of the water company and the disclosures of the ownership of the water-works by government officials, led to serious complications. Mr. Wade had been a law partner of O. H. Clark, and the firm was at once dissolved. This caused a split in the political ring, and it was plainly to be seen that Fred C. Wade, Judge Craig and Major Wood locked horns with O. H. Clark, Governor Ogilvie and Judge Dugas (who was sent in again soon after this exposure), and a few other smaller fish, and were determined to stand firm for the rights of the citizens of the Territory.

In a few days the city council met and the corrupt ring having the majority on their side passed an ordinance that the water-house should stand, thus flinging the gauntlet at the feet of the Canadian Court of Justice. The troops as well as the Northwest Mounted Police were a fine lot of fellows and were in sympathy with the people, but, lacking instructions or orders from the government at Ottawa, were unable to interfere in any way.

Knowing this state of affairs and having confidence in the Minister of Justice at Ottawa, I laid a plan of action. I began by first going to Governor Ogilvie, giving him facts to which he seemed to listen favorably. I suggested to him that the Yukon Council should meet at my hotel and I would have Mr. Wade there. I thought some satisfactory arrangements could be agreed upon to have the water-house removed. He assented promptly and they all came to my hotel the following afternoon. I noticed while they were there that there were two factions in the council. I was led to believe, however, that everything was amicably settled and that the water-house would be removed at an early date.

They adjourned to the street in front of the water-house and had barely reached the sidewalk when there arose such a row that going to the windows I saw that a fight had begun. Some young Conservatives got out the following lines which explains the whole thing.

The government newspaper organ was ready to publish these verses, but O. H. Clark, lawyer for the Canadian Bank of Commerce, and "political boss," put his oar in and threatened with arrest any one who circulated this lampoon. While Swinehart, the editor, "took water" the boys had about 6,000 copies like this typewritten and sent them through Canada.

### WHO STRUCK "BILLY"
#### OR
##### THE OPEN COUNCIL MEETING

The snow had fallen softly, the streets were still and white,
When Ogilvie and F. C. Wade met in a bloody fight,

And all the people stood aghast as clashed the warriors twain,
And not a man but hoped and prayed that they would clash again.

For Wade was known as "Fighting Fred," and Bill a Doughty Man,
An Indian fighter of renown, one of a Scottish clan,
And Dawson stood and shivered as the Council met in town,
And "Bill" eased his suspenders up, and Wade took off his gown.

My children, t'was a dreadful fight, two blows were struck in all,
They fought with skill at distant range, and neither had a fall,
And "Fred the Fighter" blacked the eye of "Bill the Western Gled,"
And "Willy" swears he'll wear the scalp of "Prosecuting Fred."

This street brawl between two government officials simply tended to widen the breach among the powers. I then saw that there was no longer any hope for justice to be had in the Territory, and proceeded to carry out my plans already made. I accordingly wrote a full statement of existing conditions in the Territory and the treatment to which I was being unjustly subjected, and forwarded the document to the Minister of

Justice at Ottawa, the Hon. David Mills. It took two months each way for my letter to get out and the reply to be brought in from Skagway, traveling over the eternal ice and snow.

Meantime the Christmas holidays occurred. On the morning of the Yuletide three young men, fine big chaps, were on the trail going out of the country, bound for their homes in the States. They were supposed to have with them about $35,000. They were Lynn Ralph, of Seattle, who was a purser on one of Mr. MacConnell's boats, Fred Clayson, of Skagway, a merchant, and a young Norwegian named Olson, who had been a lineman for the telegraph company and who unfortunately overtook the other two and traveled with them up the river trail on the ice.

They had stayed all night at the Minto Roadhouse about half way out. They were now on the last half of their long, cold journey on foot. The thermometer was 56 degrees below zero, and the cold was bitter.

About ten o'clock on Christmas morning they were enticed, or, more likely, driven, into the woods up a narrow trail which led toward a tent that was pitched in the woods out of sight of the river trail. They were all three murdered and their bodies put into the Yukon River through a hole that had been cut in the ice, which was six feet thick at that point.

They disappeared, and no one could be found who knew anything about them. The authorities said they had been seen by a policeman going up Stewart River to a new strike, and as there were rumors of a new strike on the Stewart River just at that time many were inclined to believe it.

Fred Clayson had promised his mother he would send her a dispatch from each telegraph station that he passed on his way out. She was afraid to have him start over the trail with gold-dust that time of year, when it is dark all day as well as night. He wired in accordance with his promise, the last message being sent near Minto, about half-way between Dawson and White Horse. After two days had passed and no telegram had been received she became greatly alarmed, and engaged Detective Philip R. McGuire, an American detective who was there on some work in Skagway, to look for her boy. His sympathies enlisted, he lost no time but started at once on the trail.

The morning of the day after the boys had been killed a Mrs. Prather and her husband with four other men were going outside over the same trail. She going ahead in her dog-sled discovered a fresh trail just above Minto leading into the woods. With truly feminine curiosity she started in to see where this trail led to. The impression was that it was a cut-off around the bend of the river, and by taking these cut-offs travelers could often save several miles. When she had gone less than a half-mile on this trail she discovered that it led to a small tent in the woods. She could see the river only a short distance from where she then was and decided that she would not retrace her steps, but would make a new trail for herself and those who were very close behind her. Taking a short cut she made for the river, and had only gone a few hundred yards when she found a man, who afterward proved to be George O'Brien, with a dog and sled crouched down by a tree trying to escape observation. He asked her if she was alone. She replied that her husband and four others were coming just behind her. At this he expressed himself pleased and soon joined the party, and they traveled several days together over the ice. When they neared the barracks at Tagish Post this man parted company with the people who had found him in the woods, saying he would lay up for a few days' rest. He then bought a team of horses, thinking no doubt he would be free from suspicion, as many teams were then hauling ties down the trail for the railroad that was soon to be built to White Horse.

Mr. McGuire had by this time reached the police barracks at Tagish Post going in and was advising with the officials who were there about the lost boys. George O'Brien was at that time nearing the same place going out. The ice was getting thin in places. He had succeeded in passing all the police stations, of which there were many, unmolested, and Tagish Post was the last and just ahead of him. He attempted to leave the trail which led past the Post and make a trail on the opposite side of the river for himself, and by so doing pass unobserved. But the ice was too soft; he broke through, team and all, and was floundering in the water. McGuire's acute mind at once came to the reasonable conclusion that whoever it was he must be trying to evade the Post. They got assistance and hurried to the scene, pulled the man out of the river half-drowned, and took him to the barracks. He had been in jail at Dawson till within a few weeks before the killing of these boys, and was let out and given a peculiar blanket and ax which it is customary to give to discharged pauper prisoners. The Canadian police searched him perfunctorily and found nothing incriminating. Then McGuire, after using considerable strategy, succeeded in getting permission to search the man's clothes himself. The heel of one of O'Brien's socks had a patch which had been darned carefully, and between this patch and the regular sock-heel McGuire found a one-hundred-dollar bill that had been taken from Fred Clayson. No other money or gold-dust was ever found.

George O'Brien was tried, convicted and hung for this crime. During the trial the evidence showed this: The three boys walked up that trail into the woods, Olson in the lead, Ralph next and Clayson last. They were about twenty feet apart when they came to a place where the timber was large and close together. Here Clayson sprang from the trail for a large tree, jumping a great distance, and was shot in the head while in a stooped position. Lynn Ralph, likely hearing the shot, turned to look back and fell dead in the trail with two bullet-holes in his body. Olson had a hunter's knife which he used in his defense. The frozen snow showed this, and that a terrible struggle had taken place between Olson and two other men. The footprints were visible and the frozen snow was covered with blood about fifty feet square, showing plainly that Olson had seized the rifle in the hands of another man and made a desperate fight for his life. The evidence also showed that O'Brien was not alone with the boys when they were killed. A telegram had been sent up the trail to O'Brien the same day the boys started out which for some reason could not be used in evidence. Mr. F. C. Wade prosecuted this case, and his strong efforts to fix the crime on others as well as on O'Brien were rendered fruitless by influence.

As soon as the Minister of Justice received my letter he turned it over to Clifford Sifton, Minister of the Interior, and notified me of the fact immediately thereafter. Clifford Sifton sent my letter to the Yukon Council at Dawson with confidential instructions how to proceed in the matter. I learned without doubt that these orders were to bring me to my knees and make such an example of me as would intimidate all the miners in the Yukon Territory and prevent their asserting their rights. After this the whole community, of whatever nationality, were to be robbed and stabbed with impunity by those who ruled Yukon as arbitrarily as the Doges ruled old Venice. In fact, as subsequent events will prove, the tortures of the Inquisition in Spain, save only the rack, were equaled by the officials, who not only robbed but attempted murder to forward their interest and pay off their grudges.

I had been ill several days with acute pleurisy and was out of bed for the first time in ten days when I was served with a summons out of a police court on a charge of criminal libel. The thermometer was 42 degrees below zero, and I refused to go to court, and was removed to my bed. There I remained for the next six weeks. I sent a certificate from three different physicians as to my condition, and they were all thrown out of court. I then wired to the Minister of Justice at Ottawa, asking him for a stay of proceedings. To this I received no reply.

The night following was an extremely cold night, the thermometer registering 68 degrees below zero. I was too cold to sleep, and I had my bed moved away from the window and up against a door which opened into the main hallway. Toward morning fatigue overcame me and I slumbered. I was awakened about nine o'clock by having the door near which my bed was placed pushed open, and through the opening a man's hand was pushed and a loaded revolver, cocked, was thrust in my face. The clicking of that revolver awakened me, and the barrel of that gun looked bigger than a hogshead to me.

My first thought was that some one had come to steal the gold-dust stored beneath my bed.

My lungs were sore, especially the left one, but notwithstanding I began to scream, and each scream seemed as if it would tear my lungs out of me. It was quite a while before I could stop screaming, I was so frightened.

## CHAPTER X

THEY continued to serve summonses on me daily, but I declined to go to court, and kept my bed. The following letter from one of the leading physicians of Dawson will serve to show my good faith in the matter and the persecution to which I was subjected:

"TO MAJOR WOOD,

    COMMANDING OFFICER, N. W. M. P., DAWSON, Y. T.

"DEAR SIR: I have been shown another communication from Inspector Starnes in the cases of alleged criminal libel against Luella Day. His behavior as magistrate from the very inception of the proceedings till now has been such as to aggravate and prolong her sickness.

"I have to say also that his extraordinary utterances from the bench and his conduct throughout these proceedings show a want of good faith in the administration of his office, besides amounting to a tacit impeachment of every medical affidavit before his court in this particular case.

"His communication of to-day ends as follows: 'In any case your physicians will have to appear in person to satisfy the Court verbally as to your condition.' Inspector Starnes came to see me twice on Sunday regarding this case. I told him that I would be pleased to attend court when summoned as a witness.

"Faithfully yours,

"WILLIAM CATTO, M.D."

Then a policeman invaded my bedroom where I lay ill, and brought a verbal message from Judge Dugas saying if I would come before the court and apologize, all the proceedings against me would be dropped. I refused flatly, saying I had nothing to apologize for, as every word I had written to the Minister of Justice was the truth, the whole truth, and nothing but the truth, so help me God!

Colonel MacGregor appeared on the scene with Dr. Richardson, of the mounted police, who pronounced it dangerous to my life to take me into the extreme low temperature prevailing outside.

Then a guard was placed in the house to watch over me, which was changed every four hours, until I was sufficiently recovered to be taken to the government hospital.

My friends were extremely solicitous about my being taken to the hospital, fearing that something would be done to put me out of the way and no trace left behind.

Under these circumstances it appeared to me that the most advisable thing to do was to appeal to the United States consul for protection. I dictated the following letter:

"Dawson City, Yukon Territory,
"April 9, 1901.

"To the Consul of the United States, at Dawson.

"Dear Sir: I have been summoned to appear in the police court on the 9th day of March last to answer for charges of alleged criminal libel made against me by Justice A. Dugas, William Ogilvie, Edmund Senkler and Major Z. T. Wood, but owing to illness I was unable to attend at the said court, and the case by virtue of a sworn medical certificate has been remanded from time to time.

"On the 4th inst., however, a bench warrant was issued for my arrest, notwithstanding that a sworn certificate from Dr. W. Catto was in the possession of the court testifying to my illness. The policeman who had the matter in charge, in order to execute the warrant, without a moment's warning forced my bedroom door partly open and displayed a firearm. Shortly after the detachment of police already on the scene was reinforced by a squad of Northwest Mounted Police under Captain Scarth. Dr. Catto and Dr. Richardson, after examination, protested against having me taken to the court that day. I was then placed under arrest and a guard stationed in the house over me.

"The constant worry in which I have been kept ever since the inception of these proceedings by the threats and actions of the court has seriously affected my illness and prevented my recovery. I am a citizen of the United States, and I pray that I may receive the protection that you may be able to give me in this matter.

"I will be pleased, so soon as I am able, to answer in person to my summons, but owing to the condition of my health at present I consider by doing so I would be endangering my life.

"Therefore I appeal to you in the name of the government you represent to stay these court proceedings until such time as I may be restored to health, or have a reply from either Ottawa or Washington."

I received the following answer from the vice-consul, H. TeRoller, who was also manager for one of the big company Canadian stores:

"DEAR MADAM: Your communication to Colonel McCook of April 10 has been received and referred to me, and in reply would say that while it is the duty of the consular officer to endeavor on all occasions to maintain and promote all the rightful interests of United States citizens and protect them in all privileges that are provided for by treaty or conceded by usage, yet we are *'particularly cautioned'* not to enter into any contention that can be avoided with the subjects or authorities of the country, and are constrained from taking any part in litigation.

"If, after consideration, we find that an applicant for protection has a right to our intervention, we are expected to carefully examine into the grievances, and if the complaints are well founded, all we can do is to *intercede* for them with the local authorities, but we can go no further, except to refer the matter to the State Department.

"From the foregoing, you will realize the importance of using every endeavor to meet the authorities and comply with their demand as far as it is possible to do so, and thus settle in an amicable manner all difficulties between you and them.

"Yours truly,

"H. TeRoller,
"U. S. Vice-Consul."


When I had finished reading the letter from the vice-consul and manager for the "Big Company" I sent a private messenger to Colonel McCook, the United States consul, requesting him to come to me at once, which he did. When I showed him the letter TeRoller, the vice-consul, had written to me he was furious. He said he had not been consulted in the matter at all. McCook at once took action and all court proceedings were called off.

While Colonel McCook was a dissipated man, he was a man of great courage and stood up for the rights of the government which he represented.

When the ambulance reached the court-house, having returned without me although they had been ordered to bring me before the court dead or alive, Judge Dugas nearly had an apoplectic fit. This French Canuck fairly foamed at the mouth as he pounded the bench and sputtered his venomous spittle in a six-foot radius.

He then issued a bench warrant to Captain Courtland Starnes to arrest me within a week and bring me before him, adding, "If you don't bring that woman here the next time I'll know the reason why," shaking his fist in Captain Starnes' face.

All was quiet in the streets for a few days. Mr. Wade came to see me the morning I was to be brought by Captain Starnes before Judge Dugas.

He said, "I think some one is putting up a job on me," and he flourished a paper which proved to be a telegram.

A few hours after I had received the letter from TeRoller, the United States vice-consul, he called upon me in company with Mr. F. C. Wade. They both tried their best to induce me to go before Judge Dugas and apologize. But I could not do it in justice to myself. I would have preferred death instead. If I had made any such surrender of my rights as I was asked to make, I would not only have done myself an injury and sustained a financial loss, but I held out for all those miners who were behind me not equipped with either the material or the money to make a fight against corrupt officialdom.

Mr. Wade had warned me from the beginning against sending any telegrams to the Minister of Justice or writing him any more letters. But, woman-like, I had done both.

*When the ambulance and soldiers returned without me Judge Dugas nearly had an apoplectic fit.*

He was pale and agitated as he stood in my presence. He took my hand and held it while he asked me this question: "Have you been sending telegrams and writing letters to the Minister of Justice?"

I asked him why he wanted to know. He then showed me the telegram, after having sworn me to secrecy. He said, "I think some one has been putting up a job on me."

"Why?"

"Because the Minister of Justice has no jurisdiction over this court. It is under Clifford Sifton, Minister of the Interior."

The telegram commanded F. C. Wade, Queen's Counsel, to dismiss all proceedings against me immediately, and was signed, "David Mills, Minister of Justice, Ottawa, Canada."

When court was convened Mr. Wade was at my house, and when Judge Dugas opened court neither of us was there. When the judge had worked himself up into another rage Mr. Wade walked into court and dismissed all proceedings against me by order of the Dominion government. The crowd outside yelled until they were hoarse, while Dugas, both afraid and ashamed to face them, sneaked out of the back door of the court-house and went home and stayed in bed for several days—with a fit of spleen.

The boys of the Mounted Police, who were both brave and chivalric, were "white," and they did not like the dirty work they had been commanded to do. They had been on guard over me for days, and when the shouts told them that

I had won out and all proceedings against me were dismissed they did not wait for orders, but "scooted" out of the back door of the hotel into the alleyway and made their way under cover to their headquarters.

The men had come down from the mines, and every one in town was in the court-house who could get there, and there were something like 5,000 standing outside. The news had flown from camp to camp that something would be doing that day, and I always believed that any attempt to harm me would have precipitated a riot.

The newspapers had been saying some one was wrong. If it was I, I should be severely punished; if it was the official ring, they should be made to resign at once.

From this time forth for a period of more than a year, under the rule of the Honorable David Mills, everything went smoothly in the Territory. Mr. Mills was a just man of kindly disposition, and under his administration everything flourished. He overawed the political ring, and money for investment poured into the Territory from England and America.

Business of all kinds was active and profitable to those engaged in it, and many public improvements were made. Miners brought their families into the country. Churches and schoolhouses were built. The railway was built from Lake Bennett to White Horse, connecting it with the railroad from the White Pass to Skagway. Large sums of money running into the millions were sent into the country by English and French syndicates for investment. The output of gold was not less than $12,000,000.

But the uncertainty of human life was illustrated by the death of this good man at the end of the first year.

It might truly be said of him:

"The mills of God grind slowly, but they grind
  exceeding small,
Though with patience He stands waiting, with
  exactness grinds He all."

His remains had not been laid to rest when the ring rascals started in again on their nefarious work. I met Colonel MacGregor on the street and first learned from him of this bereavement.

He said, "What are we going to do now? Our friend has passed beyond."

I said, "Who?"

"The beloved Honorable David Mills," he replied.

I was told he died suddenly as he arose from the table after partaking of a hearty meal at an official dinner.

In a few days thereafter a man came to my office and presented a note of Mr. Edward MacConnell's for $14,000, over two years past due. The note had been settled and a receipt given for the same, saying the note had been lost in a fire which had occurred about that time.

Mr. MacConnell had left the Territory and had gone on a two-years' exploring expedition several thousand miles in the interior of Alaska, making it impossible to communicate with him.

The man was a collector for the Canadian Bank of Commerce, and they owned the note.

I had bought the hotel property from Mr. MacConnell after the hotel was built, and then I took a patent on the land upon which it stood in my own name from the government at Ottawa.

This man did not claim to me that I was legally responsible on this note, as I had never seen the note. But he did urge me confidentially and as a friend to pay the note, for which he said the bank would accept $10,000, in lieu of its face value, which was $14,000.

"O. H. Clark, lawyer, and the Canadian Bank of Commerce," he said, "now that Mr. Mills has passed away, are the government, and they can and will involve you in litigation and make it cost you a good deal more than $10,000."

I had confidence in the government at Ottawa at this time. I afterward testified to this conversation in court, telling O. H. Clark he could not force me to pay this, as I never had and never intended to violate any of the laws, and I did not owe one dollar in the country, had always paid my honest debts and always expected to. I told the court I would simply stand pat and die before I would be blackmailed in this way out of a single cent.

O. H. Clark then started in to break the patent on my land. He began suit to that end and served the summons of complaint on me.

He put a *lis pendens* on the hotel property,

and served a so-called legal notice on me to raise the hotel a foot higher from the ground. They raised my assessment on the hotel from $50,000 to $80,000.

About this time the French syndicate operating in the Territory offered me $40,000 for the hotel. Knowing of the restraining order I said I could not give a valid title to the property. Mr. De Journal, a French lawyer for the French syndicate, told me that if I could put the deed on record before O. H. Clark discovered the fact that he was at fault in his law, and should have put a *caveat* instead of a *lis pendens* on the property, I could give a valid title.

The deed was drawn at once in the office of the register of deeds, who was also a Frenchman. All the clerks in the office were put to work at once. Some tale-bearer carried the news to O. H. Clark as soon as we entered the office. Presently some one was heard running through the hallway. It was O. H. Clark's confidential clerk, Stackpool, as pale as a ghost and out of breath. He absolutely threw himself through the door into the registrar's office. Just as De Journal, the French syndicate lawyer, handed me the $40,000, Stackpool excitedly threw down a *caveat* on the recorder's desk, saying, "Record that at once." Mr. Joureau, the recorder, put on his glasses, carefully read the document, keeping his good eye on the clerk, then told him he was too late. The title to the property had passed from me to the "Syndicate Lyonnaise du Klondike"; O. H. Clark's villainy had been foiled by the Frenchmen's lawyer, De Journal.

But while this "ower-true tale" reeks of villainy, life had its amusing features.

I went to my apartments in the hotel and turned my broadcloth dress-skirt into a savings bank. I sewed the $40,000 into the lining of my dress-skirt and covered it with a heavy facing of canvas, so that my heels should not wear a hole in the lining and let out my treasure. I wore the skirt day and night, never daring to take it off, allowing no one to know the place of hiding.

Added to this is the fact that I had shortly before taken a miner by the name of Brushé, who had been intoxicated for several days, spending his money recklessly, to the bank and got him to send $800 home to his wife to pay off a mortgage which he had told me was on his home in Canada. I wrote a letter to his wife telling her I had sent her $800 by draft through the Canadian Bank of Commerce. I got the draft myself and paid into the bank $800. But when she received it it was only $600. I went to the bank to report this to the manager.

I stepped into the private office of Cameron, the manager, who had taken Mr. Wills's place. This man, D. A. Cameron, was as cold-blooded as a fish and as tricky as an educated monkey. He had left a letter open on his desk that he had undoubtedly not finished reading. As I stood there waiting for him to step in from an adjoining room I noticed the letter was a private one addressed to O. H. Clark, and I read it. It was giving Clark a severe reprimand for allowing another petition to be sent in by a miner asking for the removal of Judge Dugas. He was told in few words that if he wasn't heavy enough to sit on that community of kickers another man would be sent in to take his place. The letter bore the signature of Clifford Sifton, Minister of the Interior.

I left the bank without making my errand known. For one thing, I did not propose to trust any more money of mine to the Canadian Bank of Commerce. There had been too many like the historic cat, who never came back, and their money was never claimed by any one but the officers of the bank.

The bank had done me many favors when Mr. Wills was its manager, but at this time I had no obligations in the bank and did not owe them one cent.

A few days after, Cameron, the bank's manager, sent for me. He was all smiles and took me into his private office in the bank and into his confidence. He told me he was expecting the bank's examiner, and asked me as a special favor to him to put the $40,000 in the bank if only for a few days, till the bank's examiner had gone. I told him frankly I had sent my money out of the country, but I did not say I had sent out the $40,000. He smilingly asked me, "How did you send it out?" he well knowing I had not sent it out through the bank, and that I would not trust such a sum to be sent out in any other way.

As soon as the word reached Dawson that the Minister of Justice had passed away, Clifford Sifton, Minister of the Interior, procured the appointment of a man whom he owned, body and boots, to fill the vacancy.

Thereupon there was a general exodus of the officials of the Yukon Territory. Each one gave a different reason for making the trip up the Yukon River. Each one, like the men in the Scriptures, with one accord began to make excuse. No matter what the avowed destination or the reason for going, I quickly learned that while the camp was left in sole charge of the sheriff, the officials found their way to Ottawa for a grand pow-pow with Clifford Sifton, Minister of the Interior. When Sifton took office he was said by the press to be a poor man, and now his little $5,000 had grown to $3,000,000 in four years through strict economy and the spirit of thrift. Race-horses, banquets, official receptions and general luxurious living at a high rate of expenditure characterized his life at this time.

After a few weeks these official pilgrims came straggling into camp, one at a time, except Governor Ogilvie and Fred C. Wade, Queen's Counsel, who had bearded "the lion in his den," the Ogilvie in his hall. One Fred Congdon was sent in to represent the Crown as Queen's Counsel, and also to gather in the necessary shekels to pay a defalcation of some $10,000 to the bank, so his choice was to rob Peter the miner to pay Paul the banker, or go to prison. A nicer code of morals could scarcely be conceived.

The returning officers received a warm reception from the ladies of uneasy virtue who frequented the dance-halls.

One judge named Craig, of age and professed respectability, I saw from a window in the Melbourne Hotel, which adjoined the theatre used for a dance-hall, stripped by the girls of all his clothing but a red flannel shirt and drawers, even taking off his wig, and in this poetic costume, so drunk he could not stand up, with his bald pate shining like a peeled onion, he went crawling about the dance-hall on all fours—a most diverting, not to say edifying, exhibition of judicial dignity.

Major Zachary Taylor Wood was present in uniform, and to the credit of the depraved inmates in this dive let it be said they respected the uniform, but not the wearer, for they braided his long, dark, glossy locks and fastened the ends with chewing-gum until they stood out all over his head like a lot of pigtails. Then they pinned English and American flags all over him. In this condition he arrived at home.

Everything was hot and still aheating. They got hold of an American lawyer, a renegade who had sworn allegiance to the British Crown. On him they pinned an American flag, placing it over his posterior anatomy. A Cockney from London kicked the flag and the ignoble part beneath.

This was too much for the Americans, who started a "rough-house" of a pronounced kind, and almost every man present wore scars of the battle for days. Even Dawson morals were offended, and the women were corraled in one quarter in small cabins, most of them owned by the government officials, and for which they were forced to pay exorbitant rents. So you see that so greedy were they for money that they blackmailed Cyprians out of their ill-gotten gains.

About this time a court of appeals was created at Ottawa in and for the Yukon Territory, and Judge McCauley was sent in and placed on the bench, and he, with Judges Craig and Dugas, constituted the court.

The cases in litigation were tried before one judge, and he sat on the bench to hear the appeal from his own decision in with the other two. It required the concurrence of two judges out of the three to obtain a reversal of a judgment.

O. H. Clark dominated this court in such an open and barefaced manner that the people arose in open revolt. They started a daily paper, *The Klondike Miner*. The editor of this paper was a young miner and a conservative politician. His first headline will give the key-note of the policy of this paper.

## STRIKE ON

PUBLIC PRESS AND PUBLIC SERVANTS DEFINED

AN OPEN LETTER TO THE FEDERAL AND TERRITORIAL OFFICIALS IN THE YUKON TERRITORY FROM JOSEPH ANDREW CLARKE

He began on Judge McCauley, and accused him of protecting special-privilege gambling, in the interest of the Canadian Bank of Commerce, characterizing him as "the bull-con" judge.

Some two or three gamblers on Front Street close to the bank were heavily involved from mining ventures, and while they knew the gambler's art, they were as easily caught with a salted mine as a baby. In order to allow them to get the money quickly to settle with the bank, for their liquors that the bank with their special permit had supplied them at exorbitant prices (beer $125 per barrel), they pulled every other gambling-house in town, thus throwing all the business into the hands of their debtors and taking the profits of the games to cancel their claims.

Editor Joseph Clarke exposed this nefarious business, and men who came down from the mines and joined others in Dawson proceeded to raid the Bank of Commerce gambling-dens and cart the money and chips and paraphernalia off to the court and deposit them, instead of using an ax on them. The gamblers appealed to Judge McCauley. He dismissed the cases, and handed over their gambling-tools to them so they could start again, which they did in a few days.

Joseph Andrew Clarke, in his paper, called McCauley a "bull-con" judge, and told how he was protecting the gamblers. McCauley then sued Editor Clarke for criminal libel and had him locked up.

By this time Joe Clarke's straightforward conduct of his newspaper and fearless attack on the bank and judicial rings earned him the friendship and backing of nearly every miner in the Klondike. He was bailed out of jail by the Reverend Mr. Grant, a Methodist minister, who was in sympathy with the miners. Joe Clarke demanded a jury trial before Judge Dugas, who reluctantly granted it, and throughout the trial made every ruling against Joe Clarke to help Judge McCauley, his pal in crime. The jury acquitted Joe Clarke of the charge of criminal libel. Joe Clarke got Judge McCauley on the witness-stand and convicted him of perjury on his own testimony, and also proved that he had protected the gambling interests.

Through the exposure of the rascality of the bank's officers and the judges by Joe Clarke in his paper, copies of which were sent by him to the heads of the government, the officials at Ottawa had their eyes opened and took a hand in the game. Gambling was ordered to be suppressed absolutely.

In order to get even with the miners O. H. Clark, the bank's lawyer, then started a campaign of jumping mining-claims, and stealing the dust after a clean-up. O. H. Clark also started litigation to tie up water rights and dumping privileges, and generally to do every conceivable thing to interfere with individual mining interests on Eldorado, French Hill, Gold Hill and Bonanza Creek. A syndicate was formed called the "Treadgold," and they forced the miners to give up all this location, where the richest ground was, to the Treadgold Company.

The claims of nearly every man and woman in the Territory were involved in litigation in a few weeks. As an example of this I had a water-right and ditch on French Hill which cost me

$8,000, and which I had used for two years unmolested. I found that this ditch had been tapped one night and the water diverted to an adjoining claim. When I went to ask by what right they had taken my water I was told by a blue-nose "to go to court and enforce my rights," they well knowing there was no justice to be had there.

I went to Henry Bleecker, an able lawyer, no trickster or pettifogger. He heard my case and said, "There is no doubt about it, there is no justice to be had and I don't want to take the case." He told me how O. H. Clark had stolen a power of attorney from the gold commissioner's vault belonging to a client of his, and as I had had the same experience I was not surprised.

Then I went to C. M. Woodworth, a Scotchman who had for two years fought the ring with the courage and tenacity of a bull-dog. He told me that it was no use to go into the court, that it was a parody on justice.

Woodworth told me he did not want to antagonize Judge Craig just then, as Mrs. Caulder was his client, and he expected a verdict in his favor in a few days. Caulder, who was a wealthy man owning large mining interests, had died on the trail. Frank Belcher was with him when he died, and he asked Belcher to administer his estate for his wife in Seattle. Mr. Caulder told Belcher that his name was on a note for $50,000. Later the note turned up in the bank. Frank Belcher had asserted that the dying man had told all the particulars of this obligation, but when the note turned up in the Canadian Bank of Commerce it had been raised to $100,000. Frank Belcher, who was a robust young man 28 years old, died suddenly during the litigation. The attending physician said he died from acute pneumonia, but it was the opinion of several physicians that he had been poisoned. On this account Mr. Woodworth refused to take my case, thinking he was going to get a judgment in the Caulder case, but as soon as Frank Belcher was put out of the way, the case was decided against Woodworth and his client, Mrs. Caulder.

This was the last straw, and I decided to keep away from the court and let them take judgments in lawsuits against me for money I did not owe.

In one case to which I was defendant for money I did not owe Judge Craig awarded $200 more than was asked for by the plaintiff or awarded by the jury. He was severely censured for his action in this case by the Dominion press.

The conditions had become such that the population was rapidly decreasing. People who had come there in good faith found that they were robbed with impunity, and took what gold, much or little, they had accumulated, and sneaked out on the trail, glad to get out of the country with their lives. A few instances will serve to show the worst of the conditions under which we existed.

A woman whose husband worked at night and left his money in his trousers pocket, testified that she was chloroformed, and coming partially to herself, though unable to move, saw a policeman named "Big Dick" unlock the door with a key and come in and take the money from her husband's pocket. She was a respectable married woman, but the government paper made such disgraceful allegations as to her bad character, that her husband took her out of the country a few days later.

A young man's body was found on the trail about eight miles from Dawson. The evidence showed that he had a revolver in one hand and a pipe in the other. His friends testified that he never had a revolver, nor had he ever used tobacco in any way. But what he did have when he started out was $3,000 in gold-dust, which was a good price for a pipe and an old gun. His clothes had been saturated with alcohol and set fire to, the body being burned almost beyond recognition. Two policemen had met him at the road-house at dinner, and at the inquest it was on their evidence, that he acted like a crazy man, that the verdict of suicide was recorded. Nothing more was heard of the gold. His partner told me that he had undoubtedly been murdered and robbed.

A family named Birdsie lived in a cabin. He was a miner and kept a cabin of small dimensions as a road-house. The house burned down, destroying the man and wife and three children. She was the sister of a Mother Superior in Victoria, who wrote to Major Wood, expressing her conviction that there had been foul play. This letter was printed also in Canadian papers. Nothing was ever found out about the author of the crime.

Mr. Paillard, the French consul, had been assaulted on the public street, by Joe Barrett, one of the bank's heelers. The only witness to this assault was a miner named Peter MacMahon. The French consul at once cabled his government the fact. In a few days a man took MacMahon around the mountain to see some quartz. Coming back he said MacMahon tripped and fell over the bluff and his body rolled into the river, whence it was recovered some three months afterward. But an Indian, himself unseen, said the man with him had stepped behind MacMahon, struck him with a rock on the back of the head, knocked him senseless and rolled his helpless body over the cliff. And so another man who knew too much was disposed of with neatness and despatch.

Some men about this time in an apparently deserted cabin about 14 miles up the creek, and which was securely locked, forced an entrance and walked in for a night's shelter. They were astonished to find there about 5,000 letters and 2,000 registered letters. These were addressed to people all over the world. In them the writers would tell their friends and relatives how much dust they had in their cabins, and in this way the thieves located the money and went for it.

I was told by a man who saw some of the letters that he saw a letter from Mrs. Birdsie to her sister, the Mother Superior, in Victoria, B. C., in which she said that they had $8,000 in dust in the house with which they intended to build and furnish a larger road-house in the spring. Her sister never got this letter, of course, but the thieves got the $8,000—and the family met death in the flames.

A young fellow, Burpee, a ne'er-do-well, whose family were respectable people in Ottawa, it was ascertained frequented this cabin where the letters were found. He was arrested and put in jail, but F. C. Congdon, Queen's Counsel, who had been appointed governor by Clifford Sifton just a short time before, sneaked him out of the country, saying as his excuse when the papers of Canada roasted him, that he thought Burpee was crazy. But it was Congdon's downfall, and in a short time he had to get out. The miners whose letters had been robbed held indignation meetings and were preparing to memorialize the government, when some strong characters warned him that he was in danger of his life if he stayed in Dawson, and in a few days he got out between two of them, and Dawson knew him no more.

During this time "Big Dick," the policeman, had been caught redhanded in Rudy Kahlenborn's cabin. He was at his drug-store and his wife had gone skating. Kahlenborn caught him on his return home coming out of the house. He had stolen his wife's diamond engagement-ring and a sum of money.

Sergeant Smith had to lock "Big Dick" up for the sake of appearances for a time, but he rubbed it in harder than "Big Dick" thought necessary, and then he squealed on Smith, saying in my presence that Sergeant Smith was in the stealing deeper than he was and that it was only a question of time when he would come to grief and get caught.

# CHAPTER XI

THE long, hard fight I had fought alone, and the ensuing conditions arising from the appointment of these new people, convinced me after careful reflection that the best thing to do for me was to sacrifice my property and get out of the country at the earliest possible moment. I went up to the mines, 14 miles by stage-coach, and arranged with the foreman to work out the claims, which belonged to another party, but which I was working under a power of attorney. When I returned that evening on the stage-coach from the mines, I went into Kahlenborn's drug-store just across the street. I asked for quinine capsules. He asked me what size, and I told him a dozen of two grains each. He said he was just going to his supper and asked if it would be satisfactory if he sent them over later. I replied that it would, and at that moment a man stepped from behind the prescription-counter and walked toward Kahlenborn, who said to him, "By the way, will you please attend to that for me?" I looked the man over and at once thought I recognized him as the man of whose identity I had inquired a short time before, and been told that he was the assayer at Ladue's store, whom he resembled very much indeed. As he approached Kahlenborn his hat was pushed back on his head, and I noticed a conspicuous scar on his forehead near the parting of his hair. I wondered if this man had left Ladue and was Kahlenborn's new clerk. Not knowing it was the capsules for me that he asked him to attend to I left the store and thought no more about it, except that the assayer must have a knowledge of chemistry, and as men of that kind were scarce Kahlenborn had likely hired him to help out.

I sat down in my private room which adjoins the reception-room.

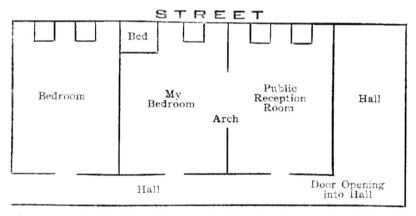

The above diagram will show the arrangement of the room fronting on the street.

About two hours later I heard a knock at the door, and upon opening it I saw a young man named Gibson, a clerk in Reed's drug-store on Water Street, about three blocks away. He handed me without a word a small envelope containing capsules. I said, "I think you must have made a mistake. I do not trade at Reed's store, but they may be meant for some of the guests of the hotel."

With that he said, "They are from Kahlenborn's drug-store."

I replied, "Oh, excuse me, then they are for me."

I afterward remembered what I paid no attention to at the time, that he made great haste to get down the stairs and into the street.

I placed the capsules on the stand and no person came into the room afterward. I continued reading my book. In about two hours I retired, and before getting in bed I took three of the capsules. They had hardly touched my stomach when I threw them up, together with the hearty meal I had eaten a few hours before. Fortunately only one of the capsules had slightly opened and a portion of its contents had left the capsule. I did not remember to have ever vomited before in my life when I was seemingly well, and I thought it very strange, but explained it to myself by thinking it was the result of having taken them on top of a hearty and undigested meal.

I slept well that night, but the following day I had no desire for food and ate nothing. My stomach was feverish.

After business hours that night, Mr. Brown, the business manager of the hotel, in accordance with his usual custom, stopped in the reception-room to hand me the day's receipts. While we were talking a man named Taylor, whom Mr. Brown recognized by his voice, came in below. Brown called to Taylor to come up to the reception-room where there was a good fire, as he was covered with ice. After Taylor had been peeled by Mr. Brown of the ice gathered on his person and his outer garments removed, he stood by the fire warming himself and shaking with the cold, and Brown told him to take a hot-scotch and some quinine and go to bed, or he would be ill from the exposure to which he had been subjected. He said he would send to Kahlenborn's and get some quinine. I said, "I have some right at hand. I got them last evening in two-grain capsules." I gave him three, and he asked me to give him one more, which I did. After drinking his hot-scotch and taking the capsules he went to his room at once. As he left the room Mr. Brown got up, saying he felt as though he had taken cold, and asked me if I could spare him a few grains of quinine. With this I handed him three of the capsules, and he handed me one back, saying two were enough for him, and after taking them went to bed.

I prepared for bed, and not feeling quite myself decided to take the three capsules remaining in the envelope myself. I then went to bed, and sitting on the edge of it my attention was attracted to a constant running up and down the hallway on the floor above. I did not think of any one being ill. I picked up the small envelope and was about to take its contents, when the motion of my hand brought the capsule between my eye and the light of the lamp, which stood on a stand near the head of my bed. The peculiar look of the contents of the capsule attracted my attention. I noticed that its contents had been triturated, and thinking there might have been a mistake I removed the top of the capsule and gently touched the contents with my tongue, and finding it to be quinine with its bitter flavor I took the three and went to bed.

Within ten minutes I felt a terrible sensation, beginning with a prickling in every part of my body as though I had hold of a powerful electric battery. At the same time a pain seized me at the pit of the stomach. This was followed by a violent contraction of the diaphragm, which threw the contents of my stomach all over my bed before I had time to raise myself up. This consisted of a glass of lemonade, which I drank when I took the capsules.

I now heard Mr. Brown and Mr. Taylor vomiting violently in their rooms over my bedroom. I knew at once that we had all been poisoned by the capsules. I thought it a case of culpable negligence, and it was some time after, and after other developments had taken place, that I reached the conclusion that it was a deliberate attempt to murder me, and that with a desire to do a kindness I had involved Brown and Taylor in my unsuspected trouble.

I heard the voice of Dr. Richardson up stairs, and I sent up to ask him to come down and see me at once, as I was very ill. He came to my room, and I explained to him the circumstances and told him of the previous experience after taking the capsules. He warned me to say nothing, as if these men died I would be in a very awkward position. I sent the doctor back to his patients and the servant down to the cafe for all the eggs behind the bar. The first half-dozen my stomach contracted and rejected them. When they came up the whites of those eggs were really cooked. I persevered, and when I got one to stay down and then another, I knew that I had counteracted the poison of arsenic, for which eggs taken in time are an antidote, as they gather the arsenic up and expel it from the stomach.

Feeling responsible, innocently enough, for their condition, I crawled up stairs to assist in saving the lives of Mr. Brown and Mr. Taylor, and remained constantly with Dr. Richardson in charge of the cases for two days and nights, until they were out of danger. They were not able to go out of doors for nearly four weeks. During this time passing to and fro through the halls I took cold, and the arsenic in my system served to contract my muscles, so that I was practically out of existence for over two months.

As soon as I was able I sent for Kahlenborn, the druggist. He denied knowing who had put up those capsules. He said, however, if the capsules that came from his drug-store contained arsenic, it was no mistake, but had been done intentionally. He promised to investigate and let me know, but so far from doing that he sold his drug-store and he and his wife quietly left the country.

I then sent to Reed's drug-store for young Gibson for the purpose of asking him where and how he got the poisonous capsules. Word came back that he had gone out of the country some time before or directly after bringing me the capsules.

It was June when I got on my feet again. I went on the stage-coach to the claim that I was working, expecting the clean-up to be ready for me. When I reached there the foreman told me that the sluice-boxes had been robbed the night before and that in his opinion the dust was then in the Canadian Bank of Commerce.

I had been up to the claim the Sunday previous to this, and had seen D. A. Cameron, the bank's manager, ride up to my claim. I was visiting on an adjoining claim, and he did not see me, but I heard him call the foreman out of the pit and down to the road, where he talked to him and asked him when my clean-up would take place.

I returned to Dawson, and the next day I sent a message to Major Wood, commanding the Northwest Mounted Police, asking him to have Detective Welsh and Sergeant Smith meet me at the office of the United States consul to hear my evidence in the matter of the sluice-box robbery.

Shortly before this I had consulted Mr. Henry D. Saylor, of Pottsville, Pa., he having succeeded Colonel McCook as United States consul. He listened to me and said, "I can do nothing with these people; it is useless to try so long as I am not backed by my government." He said he was going to resign. Shortly after, this honorable, brainy man did resign and left the Yukon Territory. The only advice he could give me was to mount a fine saddle-horse I owned and ride him some 80 miles across the line into the jungles of the American territory and thus escape the service of a capias for the last fraudulent judgment which they had secured through the courts against me. They had robbed several Americans, and then put them in jail and held them for judgments obtained by fraud until their friends came in and paid them, thus securing their release.

When I reached the consul's office I found Thomas McGowan, the lawyer for the Northern Commercial Company's stores, in charge. He told me Mr. Saylor had resigned and that he had been appointed to fill the vacancy. I found Detective Welsh and Sergeant Smith awaiting me as promised by Major Wood. The consul, McGowan, stepped out, but left his stenographer, a Miss Butts, to take the evidence. As I proceeded with my testimony I told so many details of the deviltry going on in Dawson that Sergeant Smith turned pale and trembled. I finished my story with the visit of Cameron to my claim, his confab with the foreman, the robbery of the sluice-boxes, and all the evidence which pointed to the bank officials as common robbers and thieves. Then I asked Sergeant Smith if they had found that horse yet that the government paper said Smith had offered a $500 reward for, man or horse or both. He replied that he had not heard about any horse being stolen. Then and there Detective Welsh gave him such a punch in the ribs that it nearly knocked him off his feet, saying, "Yes, you have heard of it, and you offered a $500 dollar reward for it in the morning paper." He also told Smith that the dust of the man whose claim was next to mine had been stolen also, likewise his horse, upon whose back they supposed they took the gold out of the country. This was a blind which was engineered by the bank's officials to direct suspicion from themselves. I listened until Detective Welsh finished his story, and then told mine.

The man who owned the horse that was said to be stolen had told me confidentially just the day before that the account of the robbery of his sluice-boxes and the stolen horse which was published in the government paper was all a lie; that he had been compelled to turn over every ounce of dust in his possession to the Bank of Commerce to satisfy a judgment that they had against him, and that he was not allowed to hold out even enough to pay his men for taking out the dump. He also told me that the horse had been hid in the woods, and that he was disgusted and was then about to start down the river in a small boat to the American side. He went unmolested, and never came back. Both Detective Welsh and Sergeant Smith simply stood aghast at my evidence. Surprise at the accuracy and extent of my knowledge of their villainy chased across their faces, and they actually trembled. Miss Butts, the stenographer, forgot to take down all my testimony, quitted the machine and leaned over to listen, appalled at such an unparalleled piece of rascality and crime.

As I left the consulate I was accosted near the door by Mr. John Quigg, from Seattle, who was a miner, although he had been educated for the priesthood—an honorable man and not afraid of the devil himself. His advice to me was to have nothing whatever to do with the United States consul, Thomas McGowan. He stated that McGowan while acting as his attorney had manipulated legal documents of his without his knowledge or consent in a way by which the Northern Commercial Company had taken possession of his valuable mining property. The impropriety will be seen at once of such a man representing the United States government and a big corporation at one and the same time. He was then engaged in preparing papers to have his conduct reported to the State Department.

On my way to my hotel I met a Mr. Beddo, who said, "Walk up this way with me. I want to show you a piece of property." He stopped nearly opposite a modern frame house on one of the main streets, and pointing to it said, "That property cost me $12,000, and it is free from incumbrance. You take it for $250." I assured him that I would not accept it as a gift. He then told me that he wanted to get out of the country. Lord Minto and David Mills had fought the ring, and were just and honest men, but when Mills died, Lord Minto could not successfully fight the thieves single-handed, and was going to resign. "I tell you that Clifford Sifton, Minister of the Interior, is a black-hearted villain, and the government is simply rotten."

Returning to my rooms at my hotel, I reflected deeply. It seemed impossible to believe that such a corrupt government could exist in a religious and civilized community, whose church-steeples towered to the skies. The result of my deliberations was that I made up my mind to send to Lord Minto a full statement of the conditions which existed in the Territory and the persecutions to which I had been subjected and the outrages perpetrated upon the miners, and ask his most gracious excellency for British justice. I went into Emil Stauf's real-estate office and made my affidavit before him as commissioner for taking affidavits. I charged O. H. Clark and the courts of the Territory with conspiracy in attempting to extort from me $10,000. I got affidavits from others whose cases I knew of to strengthen the indictment. I got copies of the court records in these cases under cover and through the sheriff, and was awaiting the next mail to send them to Lord Minto at Ottawa.

About this time Captain Thomas Howard, an old war-horse in the Riel rebellion, who was a guest in the Melbourne Hotel, where I was still staying, and who owned a concession on Indian River, had told me it had been given to him by the government; that it was his plum which he had demanded and received from Clifford Sifton, Minister of the Interior. The concession had prospected well, and he had been offered $240,000 for the property, which, as he told me, the government wanted him to turn back, but, said he, "I will never do it." One morning he made ready and started in a two-horse conveyance to his property in company with Captain Norwood, who was representing Mr. Laurier, Prime Minister of Canada, in the mines, and a strange man who Howard told me was represented to him as being a civil engineer. They wanted him to point out the boundary lines of his property, and had promised him the money as soon as the conveyance could be arranged.

It was about sixty miles from Dawson to the Indian River concession, which lay in the interior of the Territory. When he had been gone less than forty-eight hours he returned alone, and came into my office in the hotel. He seemed very much agitated about something. I said to him, "Captain, you surely have not been to Indian River and back so soon?"

He replied, "No. I want to tell you something. I think those people were taking me out there to kill me. I did not like the looks of that strange man, and do not believe he is a civil engineer."

I told him surely it could not be so bad as that.

He replied, "Ah, I am older than you are and am on to all such tricks. I got suspicious and came back, leaving them at a road-house."

In about three weeks Captain Thomas Howard received a telegram saying if he could come to the Russ House, in San Francisco, the deal for his concession could be consummated. I saw the telegram. He went forthwith. He landed safely at the Russ House, and shortly after, one evening, stepped out of the hotel to call upon a young physician who he told a friend had just come from Dawson. He was never seen alive again. His dead body was found in an alley behind a livery-barn two miles away from the Russ House.

## CHAPTER XII

AT this time I had about recovered from the effects of the attempt to poison me with arsenic, and was in my usual good health. My height was five feet six inches, and my weight was 168 pounds; and I was in my 38th year.

On the evening of the seventh of July, the mail being due to go out on the following afternoon, I retired at my usual hour and went to sleep almost as soon as my head touched the pillow. Between two and three o'clock A. M. I found myself trying to call Eddie Fahey, the night clerk. I smelled strongly of chloroform and was so much under the influence of it that I could hardly get out of bed and stand on my feet. When I put my hand on the fox robe I found it wet near my chin. I made my way to the door with difficulty and rang the bell, and the night clerk came. I unbolted and unlatched the door. The bolt was a stout one for obvious reasons.

I asked Eddie if he was using any chloroform liniment, and he said no and that he had none in his possession. I then told him to look through the rooms and see if any one had been using it, as they must have left the cork out of the bottle. He did so and reported to me that the only place he smelled it was as it came out of my room. By this time I had recognized, as I was a physician, the coming upon me of a chloroform chill. I sent

Eddie Fahey for Mrs Hammell, my nearest neighbor, and then for Dr. Richardson. Mrs. Hammell came at once, but Dr. Richardson was out on a case and could not be found. He then went for Dr. Sutherland. His wife told him the doctor, who was only a young physician, had gone to the United States on professional business, and that he would be back just as soon as he could make the journey, which took about three weeks. She volunteered to send a doctor, and sent her husband's partner, Dr. Arthur F. Edwards. He was physician to the government and had charge of a hospital. Dr. Sutherland got back in three weeks.

In the course of half an hour he came into the hotel and into my room. He placed his hat on a stand near the door and pulled his hair down over his brows. His swarthy complexion, flat nose and jet-black Van Dyke beard showed more than a trace of Indian blood. He came over and said, "Well, what's the matter?" in a gruff voice. He sat down on the side of the bed, and Mrs. Hammell was standing at the foot of the bed watching me. All this time I was scanning his face and feeling almost sure that he was the man I had seen in the drug-store the night the poisoned capsules were put up and sent to me and which so nearly ended three lives.

"What is your name?" I said.

He replied, "My name is Dr. Edwards," and taking a capsule from his vest-pocket was in the act of giving it to me. I kept thinking all this time, This must be the same man. As he presented the capsule I pushed the hair off his brow with a quick movement, and as I had expected there was the tell-tale scar on his forehead. He jumped back and began angrily pacing the floor. I said to Mrs. Hammell, "I don't think I need any medicine. Won't you please send down stairs and get me a strong cup of coffee?"

At this he seemed greatly offended and reprimanded me for sending for him in the night and then refusing to take his medicine. I asked his pardon for refusing the capsule. He seemed so much offended that I thought I must be mistaken in the man after all. I said, "You know, doctor, that I am a physician myself, and we doctors never like to take medicine if we can avoid it."

He said, "If you wanted a cafe man why didn't you send for one and not waste my time by sending for me at any such hour?"

I said, "Doctor, can't you give me something hypodermically to quiet my stomach?"

"Yes," he said, "I can."

I sent Eddie for a glass of water and said, "Here, doctor, you can prepare it here on this little table at my bedside."

He continued to pace the floor as though in a deep study. When Eddie brought the water he took a small morocco hypodermic case out of his vest-pocket, and then from a glass tube he took a small tablet which he said was, and I recognized it to be, one-eighth grain morphine and one-sixteenth grain atropine, which he gave me. He then left the room. Mrs. Hammell went home, leaving me feeling much relieved, as it quieted my stomach.

As soon as they were gone I called Eddie and said, "Who was that man?"

He said, "I don't know, I never saw him before."

I said, "I think that man was Ladue's assayer and the man who figured as Kahlenborn's new clerk in the drug-store where I got the capsules." I told Eddie to go and get Jack McNeeley, the proprietor of the cafe, as I felt sure he would know him.

Jack came up and assured me that the man was Dr. Edwards, who was the candidate for member of the Yukon Council (they had got representation in the Territory by this time) at the election, against Cresswell, the people's candidate. It was decided a tie between the two candidates. O. H. Clark, political boss, had the deciding vote. Of course, Cresswell was counted out, giving the office to his man, Dr. Edwards.

I was puzzling my brain as to what could be Dr. Edwards's motive in attempting my life, as I had never seen him to know him, when one of my regular physicians and friends dropped in to say goodbye, having heard I expected to leave the country in a few days. He asked me plainly, "Did you ever find out about those capsules?"

I said, "No, but I shall always think it was the mistake of the druggist."

He told me then that if I would promise not to use his name in the matter, he would tell me something. I replied, "Go ahead. What is it you know?"

He said, "I understand Dr. Edwards put up the capsules."

At that I said, "My goodness, doctor, you don't suppose that any physician who had taken the Esculapian oath, as I had done, would do such a thing, and particularly to another physician?"

As I said this he jumped to his feet and grabbing up his hat left the room, saying, "Oh, no, no," as he left, "but he might tell you what he did with them after he prepared them and how they came to be delivered by young Gibson instead of Kahlenborn's own clerk."

After a while I sent for Mrs. Hammell, and for the first time told her the exact story of the capsules at the time all three of us were sick.

"Do you suppose that Edwards would do a thing of that kind?" I asked.

"Oh, no, no, because he is a prominent member of the Presbyterian Church."

It was about half past nine o'clock of the morning after he had been there at three A. M. when I sent for him and asked Mrs. Hammell to remain to witness the conference. I had eaten a hearty breakfast (notwithstanding my misadventure) sent me from the cafe, and had been up and around my room and the halls of the hotel. I was dressed in my broadcloth skirt slipped on over my fancy nightdress with elbow flowing sleeves.

I sat in the bed while I ate my breakfast, as had been my usual custom when the mornings were cold, and was talking with Mrs. Hammell when from the window we saw Dr. Edwards coming. He met Dr. Strong, the veterinary surgeon for the government, and after talking a few moments they crossed the street and disappeared in Dr. Strong's office. In about fifteen minutes we heard him coming up-stairs. He came in and, as before, put his hat on the stand by the door. As he came into the reception-room he gave me one sharp glance, as I sat in the bed in the adjoining room. He did not speak to me, but crossed the room and exchanged a few words with Mrs. Hammell, who was also in the reception-room.

Having done this he started into my bedroom. He stopped immediately under the arch; he seemed engaged in an argument with himself.

He was deadly pale and excited, controlling himself with an effort. As he stood there I saw that his right and left arms were held tightly at his side, the left hand open and the right one closed over something, as if to conceal it, the thumb projecting. As he stood there he had the look of a guilty man, and the conviction was forced on me that I had not been mistaken, and that he was both a villain and a coward who would attack a woman. I thought quickly, I must not show that I am suspicious of him, so I will smile and say pleasantly, "Good-morning, doctor," which I did. He did not reply to my greeting; he turned his head and his eyes swept the room to see how far Mrs. Hammell was from him and her point of view. He gathered himself together and took three steps, which brought him close up to my bedside where I was sitting. I said, "Doctor, I do not need any hypodermic, but I want to ask you something." The expression of his face was indescribable. Mrs. Hammell followed him in and stood at the foot of the bed, her right hand resting on it. We were for a few seconds looking into each other's eyes, then his mouth closed tight, his nostrils expanded, his forehead went up and the pupils of his eyes dilated extraordinarily. Then he disclosed the hypodermic syringe in his right hand. Standing over me he made a vicious stab at the fleshy part of my arm. I was too quick for him and dodged, but the needle entered the back part of my forearm near my wrist. I felt the contents of the syringe, which was seemingly about half loaded. It was leaking as the needle had struck the muscular portion of the arm and would not work well. I instantly yerked the needle out and attempted to bite out the grape-like protuberance which immediately swelled up on my arm, and I tasted Fowler's solution of arsenic.

He was trembling like an aspen leaf; he shook from head to foot. He grabbed his hat and passed through the open door into the hall. He paused a second at the head of the stairs and looked back at me, expecting no doubt to see me fall back dead, and then plunged down the staircase. I knew Fowler's solution of arsenic was the main ingredient in the liquid he had injected into my veins, but subsequently other symptoms developed which showed that the liquid contained cyanide of potassium also. I was sure I was right in recognizing the large syringe used by Dr. Strong, the veterinary surgeon, on horses with the glanders, and which he had shown me a short time before when I consulted him about a favorite horse of mine.

Oh, the horror of it! Oh, the inhumanity of it! Oh, the brutality of it! It was worse than any torture inflicted by the most savage Indians on the early settlers. The Spanish Inquisition was more merciful, though ruder.

Here was a citizen, physician and official of Great Britain under the flag of St. George, murdering a woman in perfect health and in the prime of life, innocent of any crime, helpless and alone, by scientific methods of torture. The fire was flowing through my veins, my eye-sight grew dim and for five hours I was wholly blind. I knew that the faithful clerk Eddie was in the room sitting quietly, thinking I was asleep, but he could do nothing but sit by and watch and wait! Eddie had gone up to his own room for a short time and was there during Dr. Edwards's crime; when he came down, he found me, as he supposed, sound asleep, and moved about noiselessly so as not to waken me.

As Dr. Edwards hurried out of the room I threw up my hands and exclaimed, "Oh, Mrs. Hammell, they've got me at last!" She followed him down the stairs, calling to him. He stopped at the bottom and motioned her to follow him down. She said, "Doctor, what does this mean?" He replied excitedly, "That woman up there has heart disease, and you had better go right home for she will be dead in a few minutes and you might get into trouble."

About ten seconds after the fluid entered my

circulation I felt a creeping sensation through all my veins like a fly crawling on the forearm. The heart seemed to enlarge to an enormous size so suddenly and forcibly that it nearly jerked me off the bed; then it contracted as suddenly and forcibly as it had expanded. All the muscles in my body were in a constant quiver. The burning of the heart and lungs was agonizing. It seemed impossible to endure this suffering for one hour. Although I was unable to speak, my brain was working overtime. I remembered learning at my medical lectures that if I could live for five hours I might have a chance for my life from the effects of the poison. But now that I felt sure that syringe and needle were the ones I had seen in the possession of Dr. Strong, the veterinary surgeon, I did not see how I could escape blood-poisoning from the needle. Then it seemed that the inoculation of the glanders would not be complete under 21 days, at which time I was sure to be in the worst stages of blood-poisoning. It did not seem possible from my medical experience for me to survive under these conditions.

The events of my life passed in a rapid panoramic series of pictures through my mind. I saw the faces of my friends back in the East, the events of my early life and girlhood, the adventures by sea and land on my journey into the Klondike on foot and by water, the persecutions to which I had been subjected and the injuries inflicted upon me; and here I was alone, deserted by all, even those I had nursed upon the trail and in my cabin during the deadly epidemic, and I thought, Great Heavens! what a dreadful death to die. Then came before me as if in the room all the smiling faces of the friends and relatives that had passed beyond, and their hands beckoned me as if inviting me to join them. Faithful Eddie sat by my side, the only one, and I could not speak to ask the time. The hours dragged by with leaden feet, and each of them seemed a century. I kept up my efforts to speak without avail until at last I got Eddie to understand the words, "What time is it?"

"It is three o'clock," he replied.

The five hours were passed and another chance for life was given me. I told Eddie to go in next door and ask Mrs. Hammell to come in and see me. He returned with the information that she had gone up Bonanza Creek to her claim. Then I sent to the hospital for Dr. Barrett, and he was not to be found at the hospital nor at his office. No other physician could be found. It seemed they had all evaporated. A night passed slowly; for eight hours my veins seemed filled with molten lead and my lungs and other organs felt as if they were being roasted over a "quick" fire. My heart was contracted until it quivered and lost its rhythm; there was a constant tremor of all my organs, and this was perceptible in my legs and arms, whose action was visible. This lasted for nearly 24 hours.

At the end of this time at about 2 P. M. Dr. Barrett walked in, and he was followed into the room by Mrs. Hammell. I talked privately with Dr. Barrett and told him my whole story. He and I both realized that it was as much as his position was worth to openly treat my case, but he was very kind, saying, "If this had been put into your stomach, I could help you now, but as it was an injection I can do nothing." He added, "I have always considered you a perfect specimen of physical womanhood. I think now you will pull through all right." He advised me to eat no solid food, but to drink all the buttermilk I could, and get up as soon as possible and move around the house.

This abortive attempt to assassinate me so alarmed the guests of the hotel that every one left with the haste with which rats desert a sinking ship, and they were followed at once by the servants. Most of them also left the country. One of the partners in the restaurant attached to the hotel, Jack Farr, of Seattle, took his wife and child and returned to Seattle, not waiting to dispose of his interest in the business, but giving to his partner McNeeley his interest in the business.

Jack Farr told me that he was afraid to stay in the country and advised me to get out just as soon as I was able. So saying he turned his face toward home.

That night I called to Eddie at about ten o'clock to bring me a lamp. I was restless and could not sleep, and he was sleeping on a couch in the reception-room adjoining my bedroom. He came at once with the light, and I examined my left arm closely, where the needle had penetrated the forearm, and which was a large hole, showing it was not a regular practitioner's needle.

Out of this hole a bloody serum was exuding, and my arm was discolored and swollen to the shoulder. The glands involved were paining me frightfully. I sent for Mrs. Hammell, and she kept hot compresses on my arm all night. The next afternoon I succeeded in getting a professional nurse, a Mrs. Muir, and she stayed with me daytimes, but would not stay nights, as she was afraid. Eddie stayed nights, and we lived behind bolted and barred doors. This monotonous existence lasted for 20 days and nights.

I had before me 18 days longer of this painful suspense with nothing to do but to commune with my thoughts, and I can assure you it was a frightful ordeal. I had a raging fever all the time. I lived on the buttermilk diet, and gradually grew so weak I could not rise up out of the bed. I could talk and think of nothing else but that man, with his horse hypodermic syringe and the chances of my having the glanders. Dr. Barrett said he did not think the horses had the glanders, but Strong, the veterinary, had assured me that it was glanders and not "pink-eye," as Dr. Barrett suggested. In that condition I could only await the coming of the 21st day. During this period my case was widely discussed, until by order of the government the police warned people not to mention it under penalty of arrest.

Dr. Edwards was missing from Dawson, and no attempt was made to apprehend him.

I sent, while awaiting the result, a dictated letter to Governor Congdon, who wrote me to send for Major Wood and lay my grievances before him. I did so, when an officer was sent to me telling me that Governor Congdon was the man to lay my complaint before.

I then dictated a letter to Sheriff Eilbeck for protection, explaining that the nurse would not stay nights and the boy Eddie was worn out with his long vigil, and I did not feel safe, although he never left the room night or day, and Jack McNeeley was serving his meals up there in the reception-room.

The sheriff wrote me he had no jurisdiction, but that he would under the circumstances furnish me with a guard, which he did, and which was changed every four hours. The rear entrance was closed securely, and ingress and egress through the front door denied to every one who could not give a satisfactory reason for entering the premises, which were closed to guests.

The villainy extended to the government newspaper. It stated that the assassin, Dr. Edwards, had left Dawson for Skagway to attend and act as chairman of the Arctic Brotherhood convention. As a cap sheaf to this his departure was described, where friends and the citizens and a band of music made his trip a memorable one. Every word of this story was an egregious lie, as he was at that moment in hiding in the woods near the smallpox hospital.

I was at this time advised to send a telegram to Lord Minto. I dictated and sent the following:

"To Lord Minto, Governor General of Ottawa, Canada. An attempt made to murder me; all assistance from officials refused; send relief at once. Dated July 28, 1903."

Meantime I was holding my own very well; so my nurse said, although I was without medical attendance or any medicine saving the buttermilk which as a physician I was satisfied was the very best medicine I could have taken under the conditions and with my veins filled with poison. 1 felt much easier in my mind since I was nearing the 21st day, the first period of inoculation, but this self-congratulation was of brief duration, for that same night I was suddenly seized with a peculiar sensation in the frontal sinus, that part of the forehead which lies over and between the eyes, and which extends down into the cartilage of the nose. I felt as if a medico-electric battery was pressing on that portion of the bone referred to. The only relief I could get was from the pressure of the nurse's fingers placed firmly on the seat of the pain, and in this way I managed to get a little rest. About six in the morning of the 21st day I began to sneeze and vomit. I then sent at once for Dr. Barrett, who came over, and when he entered my room, he stopped, looked me over and shook his head. I interpreted this to mean that he had been encouraging me. I was right, and I was really inoculated with glanders; the fatal needle had told its tale, and as in all ages "murder will out."

I was expectorating quarts—by that I don't mean pints or less—of a peculiar mucus which was in substance like the white of eggs which had been beaten to a foam stiff enough to stand alone. It was mixed with a tint of green. The white was so white that it would have made snow look dark-

## The Tragedy of the Klondike

colored. Every physician in Dawson (four others) was at this time in attendance, and all agreed they had never seen anything like it and were at a loss to account for it. All were agreed however that whatever it was it came from my glands. Naturally I was frightened and demanded of Dr. Barrett if I hadn't a chance. He replied, "I think your strong constitution will throw it off, if you keep up your courage."

Dr. Barrett then left, while the others remained in the room. Dr. Thompson asked me what I would like to have done with Dr. Edwards. I replied I would like to have him brought back and make him tell who hired him to murder me. In a few moments Dr. Catto, the Scotchman, began laughing immoderately. The other doctors looked at him in astonishment, and I was inclined to be offended. I asked him what there was funny in a case like mine.

"Why!" he almost shouted, "to think of what they did to you and you would not die. You're going to get well, and if they shoot at you you'll catch the bullets in your hand."

Dr. Barrett's opinion was that if the needle was infected with glanders virus I would have died inside nine days. Dr. Willis Everett was an American scientist who was in the country for the Smithsonian Institution. He differed firmly but politely, saying that the solution, which undoubtedly contained Fowler's solution of arsenic and cyanide of potassium, would kill the germ of glanders.

This discharge from the glands continued

until the 28th day, when it ceased, and the strength which had sustained me on a diet of buttermilk only gave out. The crisis of the blood-poisoning was reached; my fever left me and then I collapsed. I was unconscious for nearly 24 hours.

Then with the kindly attention of my nurse and my physicians the tedious journey back to health was undertaken. Two months from the day of the assault I essayed to leave my bed, but was astonished to find how weak I was. The tendons of my lower limbs were almost powerless. I lived on bread and buttermilk and strong soups, and it was weeks before I could take, retain and digest a particle of solid food. I had lost during this time 48 pounds of flesh, and while I could stand up, I could not pick my feet up, and so had to shuffle along and hold onto the furniture. In the street I used a stick, and would sometimes lose my equilibrium and stagger like a drunken sailor.

The first day I was placed on the porch to enjoy a sun bath several things happened. Charley Thebo came to see me and brought the news of the street. He told me that an investigation committee had reached Dawson from Ottawa. Whether this was in response to my telegram, the receipt of which had been briefly acknowledged by wire but nothing more, or to the numerous petitions for an investigating committee sent to Lord Minto by the miners, I never found out. He also told me that Dr. Edwards had been seen on the streets the previous night, having left his hiding-place. Thebo assured me that the authorities would take care of Dr. Edwards, because the investigating committee was in, and I had nothing to fear henceforth. The guards had been removed from my house and Eddie and myself were there alone.

Dr. Everett had warned me not to eat a mouthful of food except that prepared and served by Jack McNeeley, and to place extra bolts on the doors, and he personally directed the nailing of heavy boards over the transoms of the two doors leading from the hallway into my rooms. He said, "From this time forth nobody can protect you but yourself, and my advice to you is to get out of the country at the earliest possible moment." He also particularly warned me not to go to sleep at night, but to sit up as long as I could, while Eddie slept, and then I could sleep in the daytime while Eddie watched.

That same night as I was lying quietly on my bed resting, but as wide awake as a weasel, I fancied I heard footsteps on the tin roof of the hotel. I listened attentively, thinking some one was climbing on the roof of a small extension covered with tin, which crackled as all tin roofs do. I counted the footsteps on my fingers, and he took exactly eight steps, which brought him directly under a window at the end of the hallway, which he opened and climbed in. The doors of all these rooms were off their hinges, as the up-stairs was undergoing repairs. He went very softly along and passed into the room directly above mine. He had only to enter from the alleyway at the back, to climb on this roof, and he was screened from view by a huge sign on the street side, and on the other by the dance-hall, which I have previously described. Once in the hotel he was in the darkness, and could make his way out easily by the same route by which he had entered, safe from observation at any point.

I called Eddie, and told him what I had heard, and he went up stairs with a light. But my calling to Eddie alarmed the intruder, whoever he was, and the sound of his jumping to the ground from the tin roof was distinctly audible, as footsteps on frozen ground always are. Eddie with his light searched all these vacant rooms without finding any one or anything except that the hall window had been left open when the miscreant made his escape. The whole house was securely locked from below. I was not satisfied, and sent down stairs for Jack McNeeley, who came up, and when he heard my story laughed at me and said it must have been cats playing on the roof, and that what I had passed through made me easily frightened. Jack went back down stairs and Eddie retired to his sofa in the next room.

About four hours later, or at three A. M., I again felt sure I heard the same window raised and the same footsteps pass through the hall and enter the room over my head. I had been mistaken the first time, both Jack and Eddie had assured me, so I kept still. Suddenly I felt myself being overcome with sleep. I could hardly keep my eyes open, but I said to myself, I must *not* sleep when I am on watch. I'll get up and move around. I pulled the fur robe that covered me from my chest and found the part over my breast wet with chloroform. I threw the robe from me and struggled to my feet, and at the same instant a stream of chloroform came pouring down into my face. I screamed to Eddie, "There's a man up there! Go quickly!" Again my voice drove off the man. He ran through the hallway, and jumped out of the window, again leaving it open. Eddie closed it, and then sent a messenger from the cafe for Dr. Willis Everett, and he brought Dr. Thompson. They came quickly, and I told them of this latest attempt on my life.

Dr. Everett wanted to go up and examine the room above, but Dr. Thompson, who was a Canadian and was running for member of Parliament, said, "No! We are not detectives!" (It may be said that he succeeded in being elected through the help of the "ring.") They left, and Jack McNeeley and Eddie went up and examined the room over my head whence the chloroform had been poured upon me. They found in the room directly over my head that a three-cornered hole had been cut in the carpet and then turned back and a hole about three inches long and half an inch wide had been cut through the floor and through the pine-board ceiling just over my head. The chloroform had been dropped through that opening onto me. This accounted for the splinters and small shavings which the chamberman found on my fox robe that was over me the first time I smelt the chloroform, had a chill and sent for a physician, and for which neither the chamberman nor I could account at the time.

Mr. McGuire, the United States detective, came to me the next day and warned me to go out at once. "Nobody can protect you or help you out. You are a smart woman; make your plans and escape in the darkness or I will not be responsible for your safety. This committee comes from Clifford Sifton, and not from Lord Minto, and it's all a fraud—they're here to do some devilish work, though I haven't yet found out what it is. But you must get out or get killed. That's all there is to it. I must go out the back way, for they are watching me," and he left me with good wishes for a safe journey.

A young man named Robertson, who had declared his intentions of becoming a Canadian, and who was a stool-pigeon for McGuire when the latter was in the United States service, called that same evening at my rooms and wanted to see me. Dr. Everett had warned me to admit no one, but remembering this fellow's association with my good friend McGuire, I admitted him to my rooms. I thought he might have a message for me. His errand was soon disclosed. He wanted to know if I would make an arrangement to settle all my differences with the bank and never say anything more about it, and added that he came authorized by the bank, and what would be my price?

Assuming even that this offer was made in

good faith, which I did not then and do not now believe, yet I was never so indignant at "the gang" as at that moment. My pride was hurt and I was insulted.

What kind of men were these who had pursued and persecuted and robbed me and would have taken my last dollar without compunction; who had three times attempted my life, and each time I was almost miraculously saved; who had condemned me to weeks of the most terrible suffering; that when with the help of God I had outwitted them at every point they should come and attempt to buy me as if I were for sale, soul and body, as they were. These "gentlemen," who were officials of a province of His Majesty's government and backed up by troops flying the British flag and bearing British rifles wherewith to make war upon sick women—faugh! My rage and disgust were unspeakable.

I told him to tell the gang I wanted none of their dirty money, and that it was merely a question of time when their acts would bring about an international complication, and when peace was made it would demand their carcasses as the sheep for a burnt offering.

Then he asked me for himself for work, saying he was disgusted with his job, and would quit to-morrow if he could make a bare living. He said, "You know winter is coming on, and it is a hard country to be in without money or work."

I told him there was nothing I could give him, not a lease on which he could make a dollar, but I said, "Don't go hungry; come to me and

I'll give you a meal-ticket. It's the best I can do."

He looked at me so strangely I asked him outright, "Why do you look at me in that way? Do I look so badly since my sickness?"

He just shook his head and said, "I never thought I was a bad fellow or that I could be influenced to do anything very wrong, but when a man's broke he's liable to do things he would not if he had plenty of money."

At this I said, "You certainly are not a bad fellow, and I have no fear of your doing anything very wrong." I off'ered him a meal-ticket, which he refused, and bade me a pleasant goodnight.

This same Robertson came into the cafe the next afternoon and sat down at the horse-shoe counter in the center and was displaying a new Krupp pistol. Jack McNeeley told him to put it away. "It's not loaded," he replied. "Never mind," said Jack, "women and children come in here, and I don't propose to have you frighten them, even with an empty gun."

He sat there until Eddie came in at his usual time, five o'clock, and sat down to his supper. Eddie left the door locked and slipped the key under it, as I had told him to do, since after my recovery I thought he would be pleased at the change from eating his meals in a sick-room. No sooner had Eddie been served and begun eating than this fellow left the cafe and came up-stairs and knocked on the door of my room.

"Who is there?" I asked.

"It is I, Robertson," he said.

I told him he would have to come later, as Eddie was at his dinner. He said in a stage whisper at the crack of the door, "I have an important message for you—something you will be glad to hear!"

I arose, went to the door, took the key from the floor, unlocked it and returned to my chair in the middle of the room, which would be about six feet from the door, and sat down, telling him to come in. He opened the door, and entering closed it, standing a little to the left of the door. He had in his hand a canvas pack-saddle, such as is used on dogs in that country. This he deposited on the floor. When I was seated I looked, and I wish I could describe his appearance accurately. He was relaxed and trembling, his eyes were bulging out of his pale, perspiring face, and he looked the picture of a frightened man. Perspiration was pouring from his forehead and his veins stood out like whipcords.

I exclaimed, "What's the matter, Robertson? You look frightened."

"I have just come in from Rock Run from a quartz claim and I have something here I want to show you," he answered. At the same time he stooped down and began fumbling in the bag. I watched him and saw the handle of a gun, which he was taking from the bag. I saw the meaning of the conversation of the previous night instantly and made a lunge for the door, found the knob, and was in the hallway, letting out scream after scream. I fell into the arms of the cook from down stairs, who heard my first scream and rushed up to see what was the matter. At this moment I saw Robertson running down stairs unloading his gun as he ran. There never was any explanation of this. You may draw your own conclusion.

## CHAPTER XIII

THE investigating committee of six which came in from Ottawa was at this time in session daily at the court-house. A very venerable old judge presided over the sessions of the committee. It was a glorious farce. Everything which in any way reflected on the government was promptly and firmly ruled out of court. This went on for about four days. Joe Clarke, Mr. Beddo, the editor, Dr. Catto and Colonel McGregor and Lawyer Woodworth undertook to get the facts on the record. The treatment accorded them was most insolent. The eight or ten leading citizens shook their fingers under the nose of the hoaryheaded old scoundrel who presided. The miners from up the creek were assembled outside, hot and boiling, and the threat of the previous day was made good, and the committee hastily gathered up their documents and fled from the court-house. Clifford Sifton had acted wisely in selecting the oldest and most feeble judge in Canada to preside on the bench, knowing that such honorable men as Joe Clarke and his followers would no sooner assault such a man than they would a dying child.

They did not stop to adjourn court, and in less than two hours they were on the steamer bound for home. They were followed by the crowd of citizens to the water's edge. And they left amid a storm of derision, catcalls and laughter, to return to Clifford Sifton and report their discomfiture to him.

The excitement was intense. The miners had come in armed, and the situation was critical in the extreme. This was the first step toward driving "the ring" out of the province, and the fighting began in a very brief time. I abandoned my mines and allowed them to revert to the government.

The last attempt to assassinate me was one too many, and I began very secretly to perfect my plans for leaving the Territory. It was impossible for me to ride across country in the state of my health and the condition of the roads.

This was Saturday, and at two o'clock the wife of an official for whom I had once done a great kindness hurriedly entered the back door and told me I was to be thrown into jail, where I was to be murdered and then adjudged a suicide and quickly buried. She begged me to get away in some way at once. A policeman came to the house with papers in his hand about four o'clock, and I hid, while some one told him I had gone up the creek, but would be back early on Monday. As Mrs. Keys, the wife of my foreman, had been with me all day and just returned, added to the fact that the policeman's Dutch blood was still boiling in his heart (for he was a near kin of Oom Paul), they were compelled to wait till Monday morning to serve the papers.

I had also been told that the shore on the opposite side of the river at the boundary line, the last police barracks down the river, was now being searched every half hour by mounted police. This was discouraging and increased the risk I had to run in getting away. At seven o'clock I sent a message to Mr. Du Bell, asking him to come to me at once, which he did. This man had always expressed his appreciation of the fact that during the epidemic I had attended and nursed him for eight weeks, and pulled him through. He always desired to do something for me, and on receipt of my message he came across the river in a little peterboro boat and landed at the foot of Ring Street about a block and a half from the hotel, but on the main street. He was on hand promptly, and I asked if I could go across with him and stay a few days at his house. I did not tell him my plans, but he knew exactly what I wanted. I asked him to take a heavy foxfur coat and some valuable papers across, and then return to the foot of King Street for me at eleven o'clock that night and wait, if I were late, in the shadow.

Jack Farr, the restaurant proprietor, had told me that there was a special watch set upon the house. He could be seen across the street watching my windows. When I went to bed and my light went out this watchman would stroll away to the dance-hall or similar places, and the rest of the night no espionage was maintained until early morning.

I left the light burning in my room and stepped into an adjoining room, which was dark. I satisfied myself that the policeman who was across the narrow street was watching my windows. I was already dressed for my journey, but I slipped on a nightgown over my clothing, went up to my window and stood there a few minutes while the policeman looked up at me. Then I pulled down the shade and turned out the light, took off the nightdress, went into the dark room and watched the zealous policeman go into the dance-hall adjoining. I rang the bell for Jack McNeeley, and he came at once. He helped me into my heavily-lined sealskin coat and a light Fedora hat and tied a white veil over my face. I took my umbrella, my entire baggage, and which I used as a cane for support. I said good-bye to Jack McNeeley, who cried and wished me well, and entered on my long, perilous journey.

It was midnight, but the street was electrically lighted. I scanned the street, which was deserted, everybody seeming to be in the dance-halls, and so, holding by a long picket fence extending nearly to the water, I was making my way to the river at the best pace I could. Half way to the river I met two policemen, who stepped out from an alleyway. I held my breath and did some quick thinking. They were sure to know me if they saw my face and my limp. As they came up I turned my back and began fumbling in the bosom of my dress as if I had lost something. They passed me by, and I kept turning until they approached and entered a dance-hall. I had some difficulty in making a small depression, for 1 could not lift my feet clear of the ground going down hill. I feared to fall and not be able to arise, when Du Bell, who had been watching, saw me coming, and running up picked me up and carried me to the boat and placed me in it. Not a word was spoken, and in silence we reached the other side.

Going up to Du Bell's house his wife was waiting for us. There I rested, while some slight repairs were made to the boat. Mrs. Du Bell gave us some hot coffee, and put up a large box of canned-beef sandwiches with which to nourish us until we should reach another stopping-place. At two o'clock Mr. Du Bell lifted me into the boat and seated me near the stern and whispered to me, "I will not be responsible for this man. I don't know anything about him. I have hired him by the month to take vegetables across the river to market, but you will have to take your chances; it is the only way. He is the best boatman I ever saw, and I'm sure he'll get you down the river all right; but my advice is not to allow him to land."

At this moment the boatman stepped into the boat, and with a whispered farewell Du Bell pushed the craft into the water. She swung around with her nose pointed down stream and the journey had begun. There were before us about seven hours of twilight, the sun not showing at this time of year before nine o'clock. And with a current always swift and sometimes torrential, when day should break we would be many miles from Dawson on our way to the coast. Du Bell's last whispered chat to me had frightened me terribly.

The scene was wild and beautiful; the high mountains on either side cast their black shadows gloomily enough over the surface of the water, but where the stream broadened out the water shone like black glass. The current in the narrower gorge of the river was running from 20 to 30 miles an hour, and my boatman had little to do with his oars but keep her head straight and prevent her swinging broadside on in the rapidly flowing stream.

There was one other precaution which I had taken, and that was to carry a pair of powerful bone forceps with me.

We glided silently along; I was watching carefully the telegraph wire. After about 15 miles had passed I espied a tent on the bank of the stream, and the boatman, who had solemnly promised not to stop at any tents, immediately turned the nose of the boat inshore. My protest was of no avail; go to that tent he would, and go to that tent he did. While he was gone I espied a telegraph pole down almost touching the nose of the boat and the wires within easy reach. I did not hesitate an instant, and seizing my powerful forceps I cut the wires, rendering it impossible for the garrison at Dawson to communicate with the military post at Forty-mile Run. I did not tell the boatman what I had done. I had already obtained such a start that even the police steam-launches could not overtake me now, and I had removed the danger of their telegraphing down the river to head me off. That was what I had most dreaded, and now nothing but some remote contingency, not to be foreseen, could interfere with my plans. It seemed as if Providence held me in the hollow of its hand.

The boatman returned, and giving no reason for his stoppage, pushed off the boat, and we continued our journey. I then entered into conversation with my boatman whom I had taken from Du Bell's.

I looked him all over, and he was no Apollo. About five feet seven inches, or a little below medium height, he looked to weigh about 145 pounds, all muscle. He wore his hair closely cropped and no beard. He looked at least 40 years old, and a more forbidding and degenerate face I have never seen.

I opened the conversation by saying, "Du Bell forgot to tell me your name."

"My name is Babcock," he replied. I had an impression when I saw him that there was something familiar about his face. I finally, after some hard thinking, succeeded in putting the name and the face together. I had never seen him, but his picture had been in all the government newspapers. Then I returned to the attack.

"Were you not with George O'Brien when those three young fellows were killed going out on the trail, starting for home at Seattle some time ago?" I asked.

This brought him up with a start. "No! I wasn't with him when they were killed. That is, I mean I wasn't with him in that tent but I was with him in the express office cabin sometime before that."

I just sat there and looked at him, my hair trying to stand on end, and cold chills running up and down my spine. The dawn was just beginning to break and I could see his features still more plainly.

"Oh! you needn't look so scared, I never killed anybody," he said.

"By the way," said I, "do you know Percy Hope, manager of one of the company's stores?"

"Yes, I know him."

I had heard him tell Du Bell that Hope was going out on Tuesday and wanted to see Du Bell before he started. I considered this a masterly piece of diplomacy. I told him, "The reason I ask you is because I gave Percy Hope all my money and my diamonds except $25. He agreed to meet me at the Rainier Grand Hotel and give them back to me. Do you think he will make trouble?"

"Oh, no, Percy is all right."

"This is all I have with me and I want you to take this $25 and hurry me safely across the line. I would rather jump into the river than be captured and I don't want to be found with a dollar on me."

I extended my hand to him with the money in it. He gazed at me with a dubious expression which said plainly, "I don't believe a word of that yarn." I held out my hand and waited fully five minutes during which he was apparently in deep thought and then he extended his hand, took the money and thrust it in his breast. This broke the ice and we bcame sociable, he asking where I was born, where I had lived, and such questions.

We reached the vicinity of Forty-mile Post at about ten o'clock. Day had broken and we went ashore, pulling the boat up on the bank and up into the weeds and covering it with brush for concealment. We lay down and watched the river. Several boatloads of miners passed, but no police boats in any direction. While we were here we ate good Mrs. Du Bell's sandwiches. I was not hungry, for I was too worried and anxious, so the lion's share fell to Babcock, who had navigated the boat for fifty miles and was as hungry as a hunter. Here we had to remain until the dark of the night in concealment. At any rate we rested, after our sleepless night, but did not slumber any, the risk was too great. The Post was just two miles ahead of us, and we had landed at the bend of the river where there was a little sheltered cove not visible from the Post. We waited here until eight o'clock that night, and then slipped the boat into the water and dropped down about two miles almost opposite the Post. Every half hour sentries from there came over and searched the shore. The river was narrow at this point. Watching our chance we pulled the boat up again into a dense underbrush and carefully concealed it and ourselves and waited for it to become pitch dark. We had hardly completed our ambuscade when across the water we could hear the patrol leave their quarters, throw the oars into the boat and start for our side of the river. Like "Ole Brer Rabbit," all we could do was to lay low, and we did. We flattened ourselves against the ground until we were **not** thicker than postage stamps. When they landed on our side they separated, always one going up and the other down the river. They were discussing the Boer war, and as soon as they became unintelligible to each other they shortened their fifty-yard beats and came back. One passed me so closely that I could have reached out and touched him. They went into their boat, and when their door was heard to close on the Post side, I just said, "Pst" to Babcock.

He gently launched the boat and put me in. We had not gone far when we heard a sound, and a terrifying one. A rapid filled the river, leaving only a narrow channel on the Post side. Babcock's splendid oarsmanship then came to the front and saved us from what seemed inevitable shipwreck and death. His powerful strokes carried us across to the channel and we swung around again headed down stream. But the thing that prevented our discovery was the opportune barking of a pack of dogs at the Post, which drowned the sound of the oars as Babcock bent to them and put his great weight on them. Had one of them broken we were inevitably lost. For the next ten miles Babcock bent to his oars until the boat fairly flew through the water, and then even his Herculean strength gave out, and he said he could go no further; we must go ashore and rest. As we were within six miles of the American line I felt rebellious, but he flatly refused, and added that we must have daylight in order to see the rocks in the channel. So ashore we went, and he pulled the boat up and lay down behind a log. He wanted to build a fire, and we had a heated whispered argument over it. I told him if he did I would crawl down the bank on my hands and knees, so he abandoned the camp-fire idea and went to sleep, while I kept watch. I am not sure I did not nap it after my long vigils, but I was awakened by the sound of footsteps, soft and stealthy, as of one having moccasins on. I could dimly see that he was picking up firewood and piling it up on his arm. When he had passed out of sight I began throwing pebbles at Babcock to arouse him without speaking. He awoke and feeling sure something was wrong crawled over to where I was concealed. I whispered, "There is somebody besides ourselves concealed around here." He rose up, shading his eyes with his hands, and after looking around carefully pointed upward to where I could see an English flag floating. He made a hasty reconnaissance and then coming back carried me to the boat and placed me in it, and with the strength of a seasoned sailor he pushed that boat into the stream and let her float down the river. When he was feeling his way his paddle made no more noise than a fish would in the water. I was not able to see into this mystery until he thought it safe to speak. "Do you know what I found up there?"

"No. What?"

"A tent flying the British flag and two policemen. Temporary camp. Watching for us!"

My breath came fast, but the promised land was then but a mile or two away, and over it floated the stars and stripes. We had escaped from Egypt, the land of bondage, into God's own country.

In a very short time we passed the stone marking the boundary and over which floated the American flag, and safe in the arms of my Uncle Sam, I drew the first long breath I had drawn in many, many months. I really felt the reaction and it made me very weak.

We were hungry, having long ago exhausted Mrs. Du Bell's sandwiches, and having had no other food since leaving Dawson. It was one o'clock P. M., when after floating with the current, we reached Eagle City, about 30 miles below. Here I said good-bye to Babcock, who had served me faithfully to the end.

Eagle City is a mining-camp, or was; it had been deserted for two reasons; first, as soon as the government establishes courts, the judges begin stealing, and the miner, who is perfectly willing to abide by mining-laws and also the unwritten laws common to mining-camps all the world over, picks up his tools and lights out for the latest discovery and begins over again. Many of the miners at Eagle and Circle City went on to Fairbanks for these reasons.

The few people loafing about gathered to see us land, and the landlord and Babcock assisted me to go ashore a short distance to the hotel.

I had a comfortable room and a good hot dinner and went to bed. At seven o'clock the next morning I embarked on the Northern Commercial's steamboat to St. Michael's on the Behring Sea. It is about 2,000 miles from Dawson to the mouth of the Yukon River.

## CHAPTER XIV

THE next few days were restful ones to me. I was chatting with a lady passenger as we passed through the Arctic Circle, telling her I hoped to reach my southern home in dear old St. Augustine in a few weeks.

She replied, "You will have to look out for this man Judge Greene, at Ramparts; he is both judge and manager for the Northern Commercial Company. They got him appointed to do their dirty work, and he does it. He holds people up going down the river and collects fraudulent accounts that are sent to him from Dawson, Canada."

I said I did not believe it.

She said, "There is something going on on this boat now. Some one is to be held up, I am sure."

We soon landed at Ramparts, and I was enjoying my dinner when a young man by the name of Phil North touched me on the shoulder and served a paper on me, demanding my trunk and all my hand baggage. The complaint said I had collected money in Dawson, Canada, for one George Sidel, who was a free passenger with me on the Northern Commercial Company's boat, and that I had failed to turn over the money, which they claimed was $400. I had never collected a cent or been authorized to collect any money for any one in Canada. I told the deputy, North, that it was an extortion game, and to go back and tell Judge Greene that he had made a mistake in his victim. He told me I must appear in Judge Greene's court at 1.15 or he would be compelled to take me. When I had finished my dinner I went to my stateroom. Almost immediately this man bolted into my stateroom with a gun in his hand and demanded that I give up all my belongings. He took my traveling-bag with my nightdress and my trunk with my sealskin and heavy winter wear, and took it to the store of the Northern Commercial Company. I refused to leave the boat, and after several hours they steamed on down the river. When we arrived at Fort Gibbon it was terribly cold. Ice was running in the river.

I was compelled to go ashore without a wrap or my woolen mitts; they were still in the possession of the Northern Commercial Company's judge.

We had stopped here to take on furs from the Indian trading-post. That night the ice came down the Tanana River and we were frozen in. Had I waited another week in Dawson, as I had originally planned, I could not have gotten through. This was another special providence. Here I was at Fort Gibbon, a United States military post, but I was at a loss where to spend the winter. It was September 29, with a prospect of eight months in the ice with no communication with the outside world. I could not be taken in at the fort, nor remain on the steamboat, so it was

"My Southern Home—in dear old St. Augustine."

the Indian village for mine. Mrs. Bartlett, a white woman, took me into her cabin. I had taken cold since my winter wraps were taken from me, and Dr. Everett had warned me to be very careful not to take cold, as it would stiffen my muscles. I was sick here for many weeks. My glands were badly swollen again, and my neck was so stiff I could not turn my head for many months without turning my whole body. I sent to the Post and asked Captain Gahart for some medicine from the regimental medicine-chest. "Ah, he was so sorry, but it was strictly against army regulations. He had the remedy in large quantity, but could not possibly let me have any." I sent to the Indian mission, three miles from Fort Gibbon, to Miss Mason, of Boston, who founded the Episcopal mission and was there for the long winter with the Rev. Mr. Prevost and his wife. They came at once and brought the medicine and looked after me until I was well enough to go to the mission, where I was made welcome and to feel like one of themselves. People who sneer at missionaries have no conception of their goodness and kindness in the remotest of places, and though I had money I could buy nothing with it, and they gave aid freely.

Shortly after this Judge Greene came down the river to Fort Gibbon, and while he was there Captain Gahart tried to collect this money from me for Judge Greene. I told the captain if he would open up a court and hear the case I would talk to him, otherwise I thought he had better stay inside of the military reservation. Judge Greene went home. When they found they could not extort one dollar from me they sent my trunk and valise to me at Fort Gibbon.

On account of these constant and flagrant outrages on the people there is sure to come a day of reckoning. Equal and exact justice before the law is a farce, and the dishonest judge is as common on the Atlantic coast as he is on Behring Sea. Lawyers in the West, as in the East, are corrupt, and the judges are in with these stealers. There is a limit to the patience of the people, and the day is not far off when this crop of blackmail and dishonesty will bear bitter fruit, of which their children will be forced to partake. This is no bid for anarchy, but only a warning to all such grafters who refuse to see the handwriting on the wall, "Mene, mene, tekel, upharsin" (You are weighed in the balance and found wanting), which met the terrified vision of Nebuchadnezzar.

About this time a new camp was struck on the American side, 240 miles up the Tanana River, called Fairbanks. Every one made the usual rush for the new strike, as is customary in mining regions all over the world. As soon as I was able I hired a man and dogs and started for Fairbanks to look after my mining interests.

When I arrived there in April, 1904, the same conditions prevailed that were in Dawson when I first went in. I was again a pioneer. They were having their clean-ups, and the results showed thousands of dollars in gold. The auriferous soil was so rich that the figures might be doubted by one who knew nothing of practical mining.

I remained here until the 9th of June, then started for Nome, where I had to stay a week waiting for the steamship owing to the terrific surf running.

We landed at San Francisco, and I left at once over the Southern Pacific Railway for home, landing at St. Augustine, Florida, the 9th of August, just two months' travel from the frigid Behring Sea and the golden but frozen shores of Alaska, to the groves of golden fruit in Florida, on the balmy bay of Matanzas.

I had made a promise to the miners before I left Alaska that I would write a book so that the government at Washington and the people of the East might know the conditions under which they lived and worked to add to the world's hoard of gold; might know their wrongs, which they had neither knowledge nor eloquence nor opportunity to give to the world. With pick and shovel and sluice-box, with "giant" and quartz mill, with all the modern mining machinery they work. Ill-fed, ill-clothed, uncared-for when sick, dumped into a box when they die, these men with the greed for gold in their kindly hearts work for others. Few ever return, fewer still ever keep a fortune made in "a lucky strike." Nature hides her gold in most remote places, and grows her grain in broad fields, but the speculative sharks of the stock exchanges get the profits. The miners are lucky to get a living, and a mighty poor one at that. A little bad whiskey and a dance-hall full of unattractive women are the only dissipation they know; but they toil on, hope ever, and at last go over the range where it is to be hoped their lot will be happier and their conduct correspondingly better. To these victims of madness which the sight of gold-dust produces a benediction, for most of them have brave hearts and hands soiled with the dirt of Mother Earth and not with the stains which mark the thief. Seek him in the busy mart.

THE END

# APPENDIX

*To the President, Senate and House of Representatives of the United States:*

This book has been written with the purpose of presenting to the general public as well as yourselves the conditions existing in the mining regions of the great Northwest under both the American flag and the English flag.

While one feels inclined to resent the wrongs done under the British flag, it must be confessed that (excepting the attempt to murder) there is little to choose between the two in their treatment of the miner.

As a result the development of the gold-fields has been greatly retarded thereby. If the claims are yielding good returns, in comes a judge with a lot of blackleg lawyers to involve them in all kinds of litigation, and through what they call "law and evidence" take their money as fast as it comes out of the ground.

I know of a place about 600 miles from Fairbanks in the interior of Alaska where about a dozen old miners are now taking out fabulous wealth and burying it, until they can get it out of the country. They keep the entrance to the canyon guarded day and night to keep their secret work quiet and thus prevent the judges and lawyers from coming in wrapped in the cloak of the law to rob them of their hard earnings.

So great is the distrust of the honesty of the judges that when a judge comes into the country to organize a court, it is a signal for the old miner, who knows from experience that he is to be the victim of litigation and robbery, and he picks up at once and makes tracks for the latest reported "new strike."

I know of camps that have been abandoned, where the dirt pays as well as ever, where only a few years ago were ten thousand miners working. Upon the advent of the court the camp shrank to five hundred for this reason.

The character of many of these judges for both honesty and morality is so low as to force one to believe they are appointed to get them as far away from Washington as possible. One conspicuous instance of this is in my mind. He took the court ten miles up a slough from Chenoa to Fairbanks, off the main navigable stream, the Tanana River, undoubtedly to increase the interest of the Northern Commercial Company (whose influence I was told secured his appointment) as well as his own real-estate holdings.

This book tells the evils; now for a few suggestions as to how to cure the evil.

Place every camp under the jurisdiction of the Department of the Interior, until it is properly incorporated and can elect its own judges. Let the camp remain under miners' law until that time. In the meantime let the President appoint three Mining Commissioners as a bureau of the

Interior Department, who shall have full jurisdiction and act as a Court of Appeals in all cases arising in unincorporated mining-camps.

Do what you think best, but in the name of justice give these miners relief from *Official Spoliation and Oppression.*

CPSIA information can be obtained at www.ICGtesting.com
Printed in the USA
LVOW061925060313

323028LV00007B/286/P

9 781177 547758